The Digital Fundraising Book

The Digital Fundraising Book

First published 2015 by Reason Digital,
3rd Floor, 24-26 Lever St, Manchester, M1 1DW

ISBN 978-0-9934773-0-0

Authors:
Matt Haworth,
Charlotte Taylor, Jordan Harling
& Rebecca Rae

Production Editor:
Greg Ashton

Researchers:
Paul Joyce & Ian Jukes

Cover Design & Illustrations:
Alex Iacobus

Designers:
Jamie Leung & Holly Bagnall

A CIP catalogue record for this book is available from the British Library.

The Digital Fundraising Book

Vol. 1

The digital fundraising guide
for charities and nonprofits

Acknowledgements

Adam Hopwood, Amy Thornley, Austin Ainley, Ben Sheridan, Ben Scutt, Ben White, Charlene Donnelly, Chris Farrell, Chris Jubb, Dan Purcell, Danny Connell, David Jones, Deepak Bhari, Ed Cox, Faisel Khan, Farooq Ansari, Firoz Ansari, Gail Williamson, Greg Ashton, Jenny Tudor, Jez Cowley, Jo Dunning, Jon DeFelice, Jonathan Garrett, Jonny Evans, Kathryn Reeve, Lauren Clark, Mark Taylor, Matthew Laver, Matthew Scarth, Milan Pankhania, Neil Redfern, Olivia Williams, Paul Jakubowski, Rachel O'Sullivan, Ralph Hardwick, Syed Huda, Tim Coppinger, and anyone who has ever or will ever work at Reason Digital.

This book is dedicated to the thousands of fundraisers who make the work of charities possible.

Foreword

As this book is published, it is likely that half the UK population will be regular users of Facebook. Not just 'registered' on Facebook - that figure reached 30 million a while back - but regular users.

So this book is timely. If half the UK population is using one of the most popular social media sites, what should charities be doing to communicate with these people, listen to them, inspire them and help them support the causes that matter to them?

Yet, nearly a quarter of a century on from dial-up Internet access from the home being launched in the UK, digital income is still not a significant source of income for many UK charities. What more could they be doing to make the most of the opportunities?

Matt Haworth's book sets out to explain and support. The practical guide he offers here is based on experience, not just of one or two charities, but many, with each of them facing different challenges. In fact, it's not just Matt; many colleagues wrote or contributed to this book. And rightly so - the digital realm is now so extensive, with so many diverse specialisms developing (data analytics, mobile, images, behavioural economics, multi-channel, etc.) that advice from more than one head is both inevitable and essential.

It is based on substantial experience too. Digital has evolved and is evolving, and it takes a certain experience of fads and dead-ends, as well as the successes, to be able to call out the essentials that charities should focus on in order to make the most of digital opportunities.

Is a printed book appropriate for a digital primer? I'm old enough to remember when printed books were the standard and indeed almost only method of sharing fundraising expertise to a wide audience. While we now have many more ways of sharing advice, there's still value in the compact and contained element of a book. Read it in one go, or work through it chapter by chapter - it is written in a format that enables both approaches.

It makes this diverse, beguiling and challenging frontier manageable.

I like a confident tone in a book. And The Digital Fundraising Book offers one - it guides you through the essentials, often backed up by data and statistics. There's also a clear progression, from covering the essentials to broadening out and extending your reach. This confident advice is catching - you read the guide and realise that you can test out these suggestions and ideas.

Printed yearbooks in US universities inspired Facebook. So I hope this book will inspire you too – to raise more funds, more effectively, to help your organisation make an even bigger difference.

Howard Lake
Fundraising UK Ltd
fundraising.co.uk
March 2016

Digital fundraising: an introduction

It's great you're reading this book because:

- Online charity donations grew 250% more than offline donations in 2013.[1]

- The average online donation in 2014 was £63.69, up from £52.87 in 2010.[2]

- 15% of all charitable donations in 2014 were made online. This is up from 9% in 2012, and 4% in 2008.[1]

- For new donors, under 64 years of age, online is now the dominant channel.[4]

Traditional fundraising is dying; digital fundraising is the future.

You need to be prepared for it.

Like the ALS Association in the US were prepared for the Ice Bucket Challenge, which raised $100 million for the charity.

You need to be ready to make the most of it.

Like the Disasters Emergency Committee did with its Syria Appeal, where 55% of donations were made online.[5]

And you need to understand its possibilities.

Like the digital campaign for the 89 year-old Tottenham barber, Aaron Biber, which raised £35,000 to rebuild his shop after it was destroyed by rioters.[6]

What's to come

If you want to learn about the tools that you can use, whether that's to get the most from social media or track conversions, then this book is for you.

If you want to track down your audiences and create relationships that last far longer than one solitary donation, then we can help you with that too.

We can also help you build on those relationships, by getting your supporters to do the hard work for you, which might sound a bit unfair, but we promise it's not.

And, ultimately, we'd like to be talking about your campaigns and success stories in the future.

So, let's raise some money digitally.

Chapter 1

Understand the basics

Overview

Since you're reading this book, chances are that you know how big of a deal fundraising is.

Anyone who's worked in the charity sector for a while has experience of setting up bake-sales, sending out donation bags and making posters. Nowadays, there's more to fundraising than the traditional methods though.

We're living in an increasingly digital world, where everything we do is slowly changing - our newspapers have been replaced by iPads, our songs are streamed from the internet instead of CDs - so why should fundraising be any different?

It isn't - it's just taking longer to catch up. Traditional methods are adapting and making way for their digital fundraising counterparts.

So, what is digital fundraising?

Digital fundraising is any kind of fundraising activity where you, or people on your behalf, are collecting money digitally. This could be done on a computer, laptop, tablet, mobile phone or maybe even a smartwatch or smart TV.

These are all ways that people can give digitally, but funds are essentially generated in three ways:

1. **Ongoing online donations:** The donations that come through your website or online fundraising page throughout the year

2. **Digital fundraising campaigns:** Income from specific digital fundraising campaigns, which are usually planned and time-limited.

3. **Digital fundraising by sponsorship:** Money raised digitally through supporter sponsorship and paid to you from your fundraisers (e.g. through their JustGiving page).

Digital fundraising doesn't generally encompass corporate, major donor or legacy fundraising. However, that doesn't mean your digital presence doesn't have an impact on these activities. Many of the same principles that you can use to make your digital fundraising successful also applies to your corporate, major donation and legacy fundraising. Rather than collecting money online though, you may be collecting expressions of interest, or requests to call somebody back, or just developing relationships instead.

Digital fundraising is more than just another source of donations. 70% of donors begin their donation research online[7] - they then may go on to donate offline. That's one reason why digital fundraising should be a component of a wider fundraising activity or campaign, not an island on its own.

What about mobile?

At first glance mobile giving may seem the same as general online giving, but if you approach them in the same way you won't get the most out of mobile. At its simplest, mobile fundraising could just mean that a visitor to your website is making a donation by typing in their credit card details on their mobile phone instead of a computer or laptop.

Sometimes though, it means collecting money through mobile apps – which few charities have been successful at, especially given the fact that you need to spend tens of thousands of pounds to develop an app before you've raised a penny. As the tools to make apps become simpler, and programmers in general become more efficient at building them, the price of creating an app will drop. So in the future, apps may become a more viable option.

Sometimes, mobile fundraising means SMS giving (text donations). This has often been seen as a small part of online fundraising (in 2012-13, 2% of donations were made by text[1]). But it's a largely untapped part which is continually growing.

Text giving has usually been at its most effective when used as part of an event, rather than as a way to give to an online fundraising campaign, so in many ways it shares as much in common with traditional fundraising as it does with digital.

Example: Sports Relief 2014

In 2014, Sport Relief raised over £5.5 million from SMS donations. At its peak, the campaign processed more than 21,000 transactions (raising £132,000) in a single minute[8].

As text giving has become more commonplace, there have been some shifts in how it's being used. It's becoming more than just another way of donating to established events. There have been successful campaigns, such as #NoMakeupSelfie, that have integrated text donations with social media as the way to give to a digital campaign. It's being used more widely as an easy way to give after being prompted on sites like Twitter and Facebook.

Rapid changes in mobile payment technology are also making mobile giving more important. Major companies such as Apple, PayPal and Google are already providing services to make payments on mobile as easy as possible and more companies are starting to get involved. Mobile payments are becoming not only a major part of digital fundraising, but will soon become a major part of everyday life.

It's predicted that text donations could raise as much as £150 million for charities in 2016, ten times more than in 2010[9]. That's probably incentive enough to get prepared.

What you need

Successful digital fundraising is that recipe you want to get right, so you're not serving up a bit of a mess at the end of it. You can't just throw anything in a pot and hope for the best. There are ingredients and instructions to follow.

Goals & Targets

First things first – what are you looking to achieve?

Is increasing your income the main goal, or are you focusing on starting new donor relationships? Perhaps your goal is even more modest – maybe you just want to top up your newsletter mailing list with some good potential donors.

Whatever you decide, make sure you set yourself targets and deadlines for each of your goals, and think about how you will measure them. We'll look into how to do this in more detail later on page 35.

Audiences

Audiences are specific groups of people that you either have access to already, or might want to reach with your campaign. For example: volunteers, local business owners, runners and joggers or the families of service users.

Divide the groups up however they make sense to you, but make sure they're specific. Don't just say "everyone". Be realistic, you're not fooling anyone when you say "men and women, aged 17-78".

So why do we want to segment our audience?

Because different audiences will be more or less likely to give based on how much of a relationship they have with you, how digitally savvy they are, how much disposable income they have and how generous they are.

The message that gets one group giving, may put another audience group off.

Who's the most generous audience?

- When it comes to gender and age, women aged 45-64 are most likely to give and give the most, whilst the least likely to give are men aged 16-24.

- In terms of location, people from Wales are most likely to give, and people from London are least likely to give.

Channels

These are the ways you reach your audiences online. You probably have a website, that's one channel. If you don't, then the first thing you'll need to do is get one. It's likely that you also have a newsletter, as well as Facebook and Twitter accounts. You may also have relationships with local press (who have websites), local bloggers, or even text message lists.

Generally speaking, your website will be the hub of campaign activity. Your other channels should be used to drive people to the website where you can "convert" them into a donor.

If you plan on using third-party giving websites, you may also use your other channels to drive people straight to one of these. For example, using Facebook updates and tweets to direct followers to your Virgin Money Giving or JustGiving page.

Mechanics

The mechanic is the style of campaign you're running.

Most campaigns simply ask for a one-off or a regular donation, but you can get far more creative.

Need ideas?

- Ask for a donation in exchange for entry into a prize draw.

- Ask people to give up their birthday gifts and ask for donations towards your cause instead.

- Get a corporate to pay a £1 donation for every tweet of a certain hashtag.

- Launch a campaign where all donations are matched by a high net-worth individual.

The possibilities are endless.

Certain mechanics will work better with different audiences and on different platforms. For example, we have found that new donors on social media tend to respond well to competitions for prizes, and donations-for-tweets style mechanics.

Tools

Tools are the pages, accounts and software you need to support the campaign mechanics you want to run.

Almost all campaigns need a donation gateway (such as a JustGiving, Virgin Money Giving or PayPal page) or better yet, an integrated donation process on your site.

You may also be using tools (such as Google Analytics) to help manage your mailing lists and social media accounts, and to measure the traffic to your website.

We'll cover these and other tools later on in the book, on page 30.

Assets

Assets are things you have access to that you can use to create more interest, or encourage more donations, for your campaigns.

These could include:

- influencers and celebrities with large online followings

- awareness weeks you could piggy-back off

- strong service user stories

- items and experiences from corporate supporters you could use as prizes or incentives

- the assets of corporate supporters

Make a list of the things you have. Doing so may prompt creative ideas about campaigns in the future.

Messages

Every campaign, as well as your ongoing fundraising, needs a strong message. One that makes it clear why someone should take the exceptional step of getting their credit card out and giving you money.

Many charities make the mistake of starting their campaign planning with message brainstorming, choosing a message without thinking about how to implement it. Most of the time message development should come last. It's usually developed opportunistically, from the audiences, channels, tools and assets you've identified as being the best (or easiest) targets.

We'll go into much more detail about crafting messages that get online audiences giving later in the book, on page 94.

Content

A strong message only gets you so far. Especially when it's all over your website, email newsletter and social media feeds all the time. No one likes a broken record - people are going to stop listening.

This is why developing a content plan is crucial for keeping people's attention and traffic flowing to your online fundraising campaign.

This content should support your campaign message and feature clear, persuasive and repeated calls-to-action (CTAs) to drive people to your donation pages.

Resources

Last, but by no means least, are your resources. These are the people who are working on the campaigns, including yourself, and the equipment they need to use. So you need to think: realistically, how much time can you give this?

Can you commit the time of other staff members or volunteers? Do you have any budget to procure creative services or professional advice?

Outline this in your strategy, so you're not making decisions about how you spend your time and money on the hoof.

Defining success

What counts as a 'normal' proportion of online donations differs according to who you ask. US-based Blackbaud found that the average nonprofit generated 6.4% of its revenue online in 2014, whilst UK-based Give as you Live report that 34% of donations to small charities come from online channels. This figure drops to 21% for medium-sized charities (50-100 employees) and 13% for charities larger than this. Whilst these figures vary greatly (due to differences in research participants, methodology, and what exactly is being measured), they do point towards a substantial and growing emphasis on digital donations.

Take the above figures as a starting point and figure out where you fit, think about it realistically and decide what your charity can achieve. At the very least, we suggest you aim to generate at least 10% of your annual donations revenue from online channels, and perhaps increasing this if you're a smaller charity (with, say, fewer than 50 employees or a total annual fundraising income of less than £500,000).

So what are the steps to success?

1. You need a set of **people** you can reach or ones who will discover your campaign online.

2. They see a fundraising message, and some of them make a **decision** to enter their credit card details and give.

3. They decide to give a certain **sum** of money each.

In technical lingo, this is what that looks like:

Unique visitors **x** *Conversion rate* **x** *Average gift* **= Money**

So, let's throw some numbers into that equation:

10,000
visitors **x**

1%
conversion rate **x**

£20
average gift

=

£2000
*resulting
donations*

Digital fundraisers are always trying to increase one or more of these three things to make sure their campaign succeeds. If you can up all three, then the effect multiplies, and you're in for much bigger incomes.

So to put that simply:

People x *Relationship* = **Money**

The more **people** you know, the more money you can make.

The deeper your **relationship** with your audience, the more of them will give, and the more they'll give on average too.

These are our raw materials: **people** and **relationships**.

We'll look at how to find people and build relationships digitally a little later on in this book, in Chapter 4, but for now, let's dig into the maths a little deeper.

Audience **x** *Conversion rate* **x** *Average gift* **x** *Number of donations*
= Lifetime value

Things start to get a little more complicated when you acknowledge that people can give multiple times. This means that you can't just judge a campaign based on the initial sum it raises.

Imagine your campaign engages two donors. The first gives a one-off donation of £10, but never thinks about your charity again. The other only gives £7 at first, but then a year later, remembers your campaign and decides to give another £7. When your campaign is running, the first donor seems to be more valuable, but when you look at the lifetime value, the second donor has given 40% more. That second donor could then go on to do even more for you in the future. Which donation would you rather have now?

If your campaign converts a one-off donor into one who gives a few times, that's great. But, if you can secure a regular donation from your campaign, meaning that the donor has committed to giving regularly, then that's even better! But the relationship shouldn't stop there. Don't take your regular donors for granted – be sure to continue to communicate with them, not only to stop them from cancelling (as 57% of donors do in the first year[10]) but also to show your appreciation.

Ultimately, you need to remember these two points:

- Digital income can be controlled with three simple things: audience size, conversion rate, and average gift.

- Success is not just the immediate income, but the lifetime value of a donor.

Return on Investment

Whilst money may be the ultimate goal, the total you raise digitally from your donors isn't the last word in digital fundraising success.

Imagine a campaign where we offered £1 to someone if they donated 50p back. That wouldn't make any sense. Yet many digital fundraisers do exactly this by accident, because they're only measuring what they're earning and not what they're spending.

There are many kind of costs that go into digital fundraising activities. The biggest though may be surprising, it's a hidden cost that's often overlooked.

Your time.

Digital fundraising can be very time-consuming. So you should create a rough time budget at the start of your campaigns. This will allow you to keep track of whether your charity is spending way more on your salary than you are getting back in donations.

Also consider the transaction fees from the digital fundraising tools you're using, as well as the cost of producing, packing and shipping any incentives or materials involved in a campaign. This is especially true for competitions and crowdsourcing, which we'll talk about later, on pages 42 and 43.

Don't worry if your first budget looks a little bleaker than you'd expect. Remember, the average lifetime value of a donor is more than their initial donation. If you can run a campaign that gets 1,000 people giving £1 each, it could still be worth spending £2,000 on that campaign as long as you believe some of those people will become regular donors.

For example, let's say ten of those 1,000 people – just 1% of them – will subsequently go on to set up a £10 monthly donation for an average retention time of 14 months. Those regular donations will add up to £1,400 over time. Add that to the £1,000 in one-off donations and you've raised £2,400. That's £400 more than you've spent.

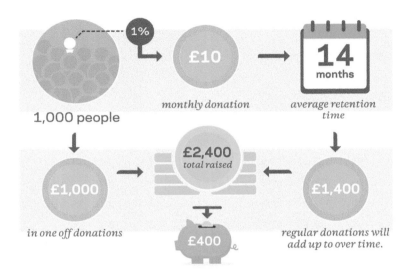

This is a common state of affairs in digital fundraising. Small one-off or text donations are used to capture a relationship and contact details. These contact details are then used to reach out and deepen that relationship, in order to increase the value of subsequent donations.

Using your knowledge

So now you know what you want, how do you go about getting it?

Stepping into the world of digital fundraising can be scary at first, especially if you describe yourself as being "technologically illiterate" or "not very good with computers". It's easy to see those who are succeeding and be disheartened because they seem like such naturals. Here's the thing though: most of them aren't. All they have is confidence, a little knowledge and some basic tools...

Chapter 2

Know what you'll need

Overview

Imagine a painter with no brushes, a blacksmith without an anvil, or a chef with no oven. Sounds ridiculous, doesn't it? Sure, these people might be able to get the job done – you can paint a wall with just your hands – but it's not possible for them to do it well. Digital fundraising is no different; you can get some results with just your wits and website, but to make the most of your efforts, you need the tools of the trade.

First up, let's see if you have everything in place that you need to start digital fundraising or, if you've already started, to start doing much more of it.

The tools

A website

Whilst it's possible to fundraise by driving traffic directly from your newsletter, or social media feeds, to a fundraising page on a tool like JustGiving, ultimately your website should play a central role in your campaigns.

You should be creating content supporting your campaign throughout your website – whether clear call-to-actions on the homepage, updates in your news feed, or on the campaign page you set up.

As well as campaign information, you should permanently feature information and links on how users can donate to you all-year-round. This will turn some of your website visitors into donors, without you having to make any other efforts.

Another advantage of driving traffic to a campaign page, or piece of content on your website, is that you get stats about how many people do it, and clues about who they are, which leads us on to...

A way to collect money, digitally

The ideal way to take donations online is integrating the donation process into your own website. Doing so allows you a greater control over your donations and means that your donors never have to leave your site.

Sometimes though, it's technically impossible to add an integrated donation form to your site. This might be because your site is old and out of date, you don't have the resources to do so, or you're just not willing to pay the upfront cost.

If that's the case, then you'll need to sign up to either a fundraising platform[11] (like JustGiving) or a payment gateway[12] (like PayPal) and then direct your users there from your site.

You should register with JustGiving and Virgin Money Giving. These sites are recommended because they have good public brand recognition and trust. In most cases Virgin Money Giving works out cheaper, and has features to allow you to sell places on events too.

However, public recognition of JustGiving is higher, they offer a free text giving service, and it's likely more people have existing JustGiving accounts than Virgin Money Giving accounts, making it quicker for them to give to you.

More than 13,000 charities have registered with JustGiving, and over 8,300 charities have registered with Virgin Money Giving—so why not join them?

Setting up an account on a fundraising website also lists you on their search, so if fundraisers want to set up a page in support of your charity they can do, and you will be paid the money directly.

Having accounts on multiple fundraising sites will help fundraisers find you, and you can take advantage of special campaign offers - but try to be consistent in where you drive potential donors to in order to avoid donor confusion.

Fundraising platforms process and pay Gift Aid for you, if you're registered with Gift Aid and have a Gift Aid number. If you need more guidance on this, the Institute of Fundraising has a whole section on registering and claiming for Gift Aid (http://www.institute-of-fundraising.org.uk/guidance/fundraising-essentials-legislation/tax-effective-giving/gift-aid/registering-and-claiming/).[13]

A report of traffic to your campaign page(s)

Knowing how many people see your campaign page, and then follow a link to donate, will help you to understand how successful your campaign is at converting your audience into donors.

The tool to use here is Google Analytics.

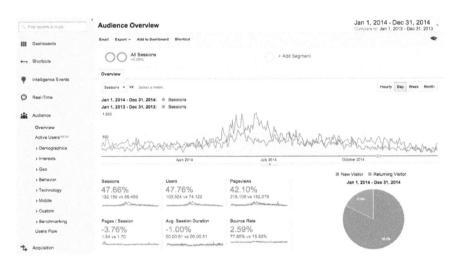

A screenshot of Google Analytics in action.

Google Analytics is a free tool you can use with your website. It's invisible – hidden in the code – and it records statistics on the number of people that visit your site, what they're looking at, for how long, on what type of computer, where they came from, which country they're in and lots of other useful statistics.

Most websites already have it, but you'll need a log-in to access it. If it's not on your site, you'll probably need a bit of technical help from your agency or a tech-savvy volunteer to get it sorted.

Google Analytics is useful for digital fundraisers because it can tell you how many visits you've had to your website in any given period. If you know how many donations you got from your website in that period, then you can easily work out your conversion rate.

For example, if Google tells you that you had 1,000 visits this week, and you got 10 donations, then you would know that your conversion rate was 1% ($10 / 1000 = 0.01$).

You can also look at visits to a specific page, like an appeal page, and see how many people clicked from that page to the donate page, giving you an estimated conversion rate for the first step in the process. If you're tracking donations by appeal you could calculate the true conversion rate exactly as above, although this becomes difficult if you're not sure which donations have come from an appeal, and which are just general donations through the site.

You can improve the information you get from Google Analytics by setting up 'Goals'. This is a feature that lets you define a series of pages that a user goes through to achieve a goal.

Google will then track how many times this goal is achieved.

You can see an example of the series of pages a user may go through to achieve a goal on the following page.

For example:

The series of pages a user might go through to acheive a goal in Google Analytics.

By setting up a goal for each campaign you can also track the conversion rate of particular campaigns, even if you're not tracking which donations are for certain campaigns on your site. Goals also automatically report conversion rates overall, and at each step in the process, saving you some maths, which is never a bad thing.

A limitation of goals is that Google doesn't know the amount of each donation – although you can set an average value as a rough approximation. Another feature solves this though: e-commerce tracking.

By setting this up, Google will give you a report of the number of sales (or donations in your case) and what each one is worth. It will even report how many pounds and pence the site has taken in total over any given range.

The downside of e-commerce reporting is that it's much harder to do the initial set up, than with goals, and will require a programmer from your agency or volunteer base to do it. It's well worth the investment though. Anything that gives you more insight into why people are giving will pay off in the long run.

These features become especially powerful when combined with something called segments. Google allows you to carve up your visitors into different sets, or segments, based on rules.

For example, all people that came from Twitter, or all people that clicked from your newsletter, or people that read a case study on the site. These segments can be saved, and then toggled on and off when viewing your reports on goals or e-commerce. This means you can see which stories have the biggest conversion rates, if Facebook or Twitter users give more money than donors from other sources, how many donations in pounds and pence come from each channel, and more.

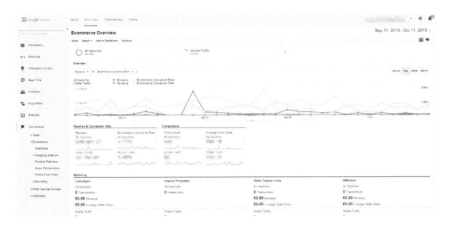

An example of e-commerce tracking.

Google Analytics data updates many times a day, so for all intents and purposes, the information you're getting is in real time. This is one of the most powerful things about digital fundraising, and it can be very addictive if you're used to getting reports on direct mail appeals or street collections only once a month.

Plus, the insights you can generate about the content and messaging that's driving the most donations are useful far beyond just your digital fundraising.

Reports on donations

Now if you don't have Google Analytics set-up, it's really important, whatever tool you use, that you know how to get access to a report of your donations. Without analytics you don't have a strategy, just guesswork.

Usually you can access stats through a login-protected admin page, or dashboard, on your site, payment gateway, or external fundraising platform.

The reason why this is important is because it enables you to see if your campaign is succeeding, and then you can make a note of what you might be doing right or wrong. But it's also so you can contact donors to thank them and engage them in future campaigns.

Remember though, fundraising platforms will only give you contact information if the user gives their consent, so you won't get the details of all users.

A way to be contacted by donors

As you do more digital fundraising, you're going to hear from more donors and potential donors. You want to make sure these enquiries get answered, as each could be worth their weight in gold.

Agree on who will deal with these enquiries, what the phone number will be and what email address to use, to ensure no one falls through the cracks or has a bad experience. An unanswered email sounds like a very simple thing, but it could easily cost you support if not tended to properly.

Make your contact details easily accessible; don't force people to jump through hoops just to talk to you. Give that human touch, name the person who people will need to speak to, and it'll increase people's willingness to reach out to you. So, where you can, try publishing a name, or even a photo, with this contact information.

A social presence

No one gets married on the first date, and few donors give the first time they hear about you or your campaign. It's all about relationships.

Digital comes into its own here, allowing you to reach tens of thousands of people with little to no cost, and comparatively little effort.

But are the people you need to reach using social media and email?

In 2012, Britain recorded the second highest level of social media usage in Europe[14] and this figure now stands at 55% of adults[15]. Evidence suggests that even those who we'd generally least expect to be engaged online are increasingly to be found there.

For example, 42% of people aged 65-and-over in the UK use the internet[16], and almost two thirds of the world's online population now regularly access a Facebook account[17], so your potential online donor base is massive.

In order of usefulness for fundraisers, the tools to use here are:

1. **An email newsletter:** When it comes to being efficient with your time, sending emails tends to produce the best results for fundraising in terms of pounds and pence. Donations originating from emails account for around a third of overall online fundraising revenue[18].

2. **Facebook:** This can generate direct donations, but the main fundraising payoff is as a relationship-building tool. It's often more powerful when used by your supporters asking their friends

for sponsorship, so encouraging them to use it is a must.

3. **Twitter:** Most charities report fewer direct donations from Twitter than newsletters and Facebook, but it can still generate them. Again, this platform tends to be best for developing relationships, especially with professional and influential audiences such as journalists, MPs and celebrities, who can then spread your messages. Every share of a JustGiving campaign to Twitter is worth, on average, an additional £1.80 in donations[19].

The ability to fail and carry on

Digital fundraising is hard, so make sure you're not dependent on expected income.

It's better to see each campaign as an experiment with a new audience, a new mechanic, or a new message. Each time you learn more about what works, you can eliminate something that doesn't work, which means you can gradually get better over time.

Don't give up after the first failed campaign. Even huge national charities have their flops. What sets them apart is that they make sure they learn from it, dust themselves off, and try again.

The mechanics

There are lots of ways people can give you money online. These are the 'mechanics' of a campaign.

Single donation

This is the most common type of digital fundraising mechanic;

it's the one that immediately springs to mind when people think of donating. 'A single donation is a one off gift that's usually paid by credit or debit card, either on your website or through an online fundraising site like JustGiving. If you currently have a donation button on your website then this is a mechanic you're likely already using.

Regular donation

These are regular, often monthly, gifts. Ideally, these should be set up with a direct debit for maximum retention, as people change banks less than jobs or houses. Many donors prefer repeat card charges through an online fundraising site though.

Regular donations are harder to get, but more valuable than a one-off gift as they provide a more consistent stream of income. But be wary, people may cancel their direct debit or get a new card at any time, so don't depend on just your existing regular donations. You'll need to frequently top-up with new regular donors.

Text

Text donation is when a donor gives by texting a special number with a code. You'll have seen this used in many TV ads which say something along the lines of "Text Give5 to 80000". In the UK, it's possible to donate a maximum of £10, three times a day, but most are £3-£5 one-off donations. Donors pay this through their mobile phone bill.

Though text donations can be used to raise one-off funds, their true value is as a gateway donation. Big charities call all of their text donors and see success rates of 5%-25% at 'upselling' to a higher or regular gift. However, it's worth considering the wider opinion on charity cold-calling. Charities' choices of fundraising methods are of increasing concern among the public, with two-thirds (67%) agreeing that some fundraising methods used by charities make them uncomfortable, which is a significant increase from the proportion who said this in 2010 (60%)[20].

Matched giving

This is a way to incentivise more one-off donations by telling donors their gift will be matched, usually within a time and maximum amount limit, doubling the value of it to the charity. This works because it makes a donation feel like it has more of an impact and it adds a sense of urgency to completing the donation soon, rather than putting it off until later. These are often backed by a corporate, high-net-worth or grant funder.

LocalGiving and theBigGive offer matched giving as part of certain campaigns, but finding your own matcher is best as it gives you the flexibility to run the campaign when, where and how it is best for you.

Crowdfunding

Crowdfunding is basically just a fundraising page with public video pitch and live fundraising totaliser to raise money for a specific project. Often incentives are offered for pledges, with rarer and more valuable incentives being offered for higher pledges.

The most popular platform, Kickstarter, doesn't allow charity campaigns. IndieGoGo is the second most popular, and does allow them, as does Crowdfunder.co.uk. You should consider the cost of any incentives you offer, the fees of the platform, and the inbuilt audience of the platform before deciding to go ahead.

A true crowdfunding effort only turns donation pledges into actual payments if the initial goal is reached.

Competitions & Lotteries

Offering entry to a competition in exchange for donations can greatly incentivise giving. Often the prize is a 'money can't buy' item or experience, donated by a corporate or high-net-worth donor. Similar to crowdfunding, you can offer incentives for higher donations, including bonus entries. Prize incentives work particularly well at converting social media followers into donors.

There are some legal restrictions to take into consideration when running a competition or lottery though. Running the competition as a 'free prize draw with paid entry option' is the easiest legal structure, but make sure to consult the guidelines set out by the Gambling Commission before you consider a competition campaign. Remember, legally you can't collect Gift Aid on prize draws.

Cost-free donations

Almost anyone will donate to you if it doesn't cost them anything to do it. Corporates and high-net-worths may sponsor a campaign with you where they donate a pound for every tweet mentioning a phrase or link, for example.

Alternatively, some sites offer you a share of advertising or referral revenue when users search or shop using a particular toolbar or gateway site. Everyclick, Give as you Live, Easy Fundraising and Care2Save are the main platforms here. Often revenue from search toolbars is insignificant, but shopping revenue can add up if your donors are committed to using the site or toolbar, especially if they use it for big purchases like holidays, furniture and train travel.

E-commerce & auctions

You can sell items or event tickets online to raise funds. Tools like Shopify let you set up a store quickly, and eBay has tools for charities selling goods online. Eventbrite is a popular tool which allows you to sell tickets to events with a per-sale fee, although Virgin Money Giving also has a good, free tool to collect event registration fees for fundraising events.

Ensuring you're promoting your charity's shops (and any other places where people can donate unwanted goods) online - whether on your website, on Google Places, search engines, or social media - can also boost your sale revenue.

Traditional sponsorship

It's not something you can action directly, but often the main source of digital fundraising income for charities comes from sponsored challenges. Sites like JustGiving are making it easier for people to collect funds as sponsorship for taking on challenges, and ensure that money is paid - with Gift Aid - directly to the charity.

It's far easier for individuals to get money from friends, family and colleagues than it is for a charity to ask.

Research into charitable behaviour among university students found that peer pressure had a profound effect on donation patterns. When asked to donate by an existing friend, an individual was significantly more likely to donate - and donate more - than if asked by a stranger[21].

Empowering your supporters to regularly and effectively fundraise for you should be a key part of your strategy.

Novel sponsorship

To raise sponsorship funds you used to have to take on a big, physical challenge. Some charities are inventing new activities for the less active amongst us. One example is charity: water's 'Give Up Your Birthday' campaign. They provide supporters with an online tool that that creates a page they can email to family and friends, which asks for donations instead of birthday gifts.

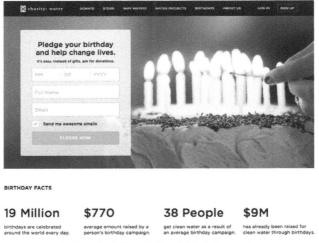

charity:water's 'Give Up Your Birthday' campaign.

Then there is Movember, the month in which moustaches are grown to raise awareness about prostate cancer, male depression, and other men's health issues. Few men are fit enough to run a marathon but most can manage a month without shaving. As proven in the first seven years of Movember when men with facial fuzz raised $174 million for the Movember Foundation.

Grassroots fundraising phenomena

The fundraising campaigns that steal the news headlines almost always fall into this category. Some random chain of events or idea catches fire on social media, and "goes viral" resulting in millions, or even hundreds of millions of pounds for charity.

For example, the Ice Bucket Challenge, #NoMakeUpSelfie, and the surge of in memoriam donations for marathon runner Claire Squires. It's unlikely you'll be the lucky recipient of hundreds of millions from one of these by chance, and you can't just make them happen however much you try, but there are ways to use them to raise funds.

The Ice Bucket Challenge and the #NoMakeupSelfie.

Get to work

You should, thanks to this chapter, have a rough idea of what's inside your metaphorical digital fundraising toolbox. But, as with your average DIY project, your online fundraising target won't put itself together. You're going to have to do it yourself.

That's probably one of the biggest misconceptions when it comes to digital – that it will just 'work'. Simply setting everything up isn't enough.

You're going to have to work at engaging people. And while that isn't what we'd all like to hear, it's not as bad as assembling a flat-pack...

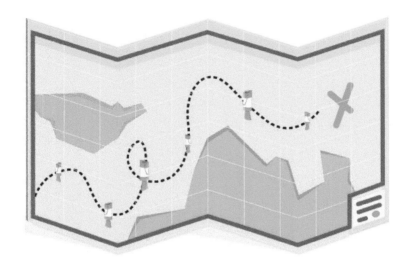

Chapter 3
Create a journey

Overview

When you want to get people from A to B, it's your job to create that path for them. It should be simple, easy to navigate and, most importantly, a path that they want to take.

In your case, you want to take your audience on a journey; a journey to becoming a donor, or the very least, a supporter. You have two choices - you can make it about you, or you can make it about them. If that path is all about your journey and not their own, they will soon grow tired and turn back.

Take your audiences places that they want to go.

Deciding on a journey

One thing that makes digital fundraising so difficult is that you can't see your donors. That's why it's important to make an effort to put yourself in their shoes. A good way to do this is to imagine, or act out, their donor journey.

So let's take a look at two donor journeys.

Here's the first:

1. We search for something and we find a charity's website online. We've known about this organisation for a while and have been to their site before.

2. The content doesn't look that interesting, because it's about the organisation's news – not what we're interested in.

3. But we like what the organisation does, so we go ahead and decide to try and donate to support them.

4. The donate link downloads a PDF. So we try and print it out, but our printer is out of ink, so we go and buy some, then we come back and print it.

5. Then we fill the form in...with a quill...by candlelight, and attach it to a carrier pigeon to deliver a cheque...possibly.

6. A few weeks later we get a letter in the post asking us to give to some other campaign, also by post.

Here's another one:

1. We're browsing Twitter and we see that a friend has shared a link to an interesting article about an issue we care about.

2. The content looks good, because it's interesting to us.

3. We decide to support the organisation responsible for the article, as we've seen a friend is involved with them and says good things about them on social media.

4. We decide to give a bit extra because it explains that £25 could do a lot more than the £10 we were thinking of.

5. We put card details in online. In fact, the computer has remembered them and automatically does this for us.

6. We see a 'thank you' page, and decide to share on social media because it tells us that this is a way we can help the charity more for free.

7. We get an email a little later on thanking us for the donation and inviting us to get involved in the charity's community of supporters.

It's clear which donor journey works best, and what will convert the most number of site visitors into donors.

Be especially observant the next time you find yourself interacting with an online fundraising campaign as a 'civilian'. How did you come across it? Why did it catch your eye? Why did you give that amount? And what was the experience like?

And one more thing – have you ever donated to your own charity online?

Probably not, it's a weird thing to do after all. But if you don't do that, you don't know what the journey is like. Put it on your to-do list.

The six stages of digital fundraising

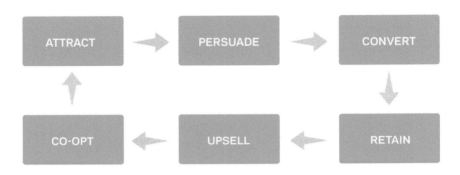

While there are six steps to digital fundraising, we're going to break them into two groups.

By imagining or acting out digital donor journeys we can now see donors go through three initial steps in order to give to you. From your perspective it looks like this:

Attract   Persuade   Convert

The basic three steps

1. **Attract:** Getting people to discover you and your campaign.
    This might happen on your website, newsletter, social media,
    search engines, or because your campaign is featured on another
    person's website, newsletter or social media accounts. This is
    something you work at constantly, rather than something you just
    get right once and move on.

2. **Persuade:** Convincing the visitor to give with effective messaging
    and content, which we'll look at in more detail later, in Chapter
    5. Every word they read, image they see and video they watch in
    the run up to being asked for money is part of this process. You
    can get this right, then leave it in place for a while, but you should
    create fresh content and calls-to-action for each new campaign.

3. **Convert:** Asking for the visitor to become a donor and getting
    them to actually go through with the process of giving – usually
    by entering their details into a form on a your website or a third-
    party site like JustGiving, or by texting a number. If you're using a

third-party site, having a clear link to the donations page is pretty much the only control you can have over this stage of the process, as you can't make changes to the forms on these sites (although they are very well optimised already). If you are using your own form, you can improve conversions by following the advice on page 123.

Ultimately, think of conversions as a funnel, with lots of people going in at the top, and fewer coming out the bottom.

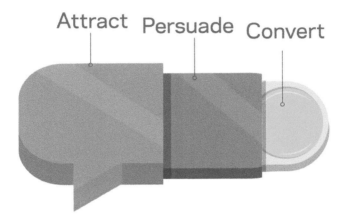

So, how good is your existing website and communications at doing these three steps? If there's a block in any part of the funnel, no donations will come out the bottom of it.

Often there's a time delay between steps; people may see you or your campaign many times before deciding to give, or they may decide to give but put it off until later. That's why communicating with your audience through newsletters and social media is so important.

The three advanced steps.

Those were the basic steps, but ideally the donor journey shouldn't end here. There are three more advanced steps:

Retain   Upsell   Co-opt

1. **Retain:** You want to make this more than a one-off donation. So step four is to make the donor feel appreciated by thanking them. After this, we want to give them reasons to give again (if it's a one-off gift) or to carry on with their regular gift. Adding them to your newsletter (if they've given contact consent) and encouraging them to follow you on social media will be easy if they've taken the step to give. Keep publishing a regular mix of messages and content about your impact on these channels and campaigns, and you'll be sure to keep your newfound donors engaged and thinking about donating.

2. **Upsell:** Of course we shouldn't just set our sights on retaining a donor. We should develop our relationship to a point that the donor will give more the next time, or 'upgrade' their donation from a small one-off or text donation to a regular one. It can feel cheeky to ask, but ask we must if we want to maximise income. The trick is to ensure you've properly thanked them first, wait

a while, and then reach them with some ongoing comms or conversation about your impact since, to show them their last donation was used wisely.

3. **Co-opt:** Ideally you want to develop your relationship to a point where your supporters will go out and find more supporters for you. This is an extremely effective way to fundraise digitally, both in terms of your own efforts, and in terms of converting potential donors into actual donors. Signing them up to do a sponsored event is the easiest way to do this, but digital provides lots of creative ways to do it too. This is why websites sometimes send you gift cards with codes for money off to give to friends at Christmas; to get you to do their sales for them.

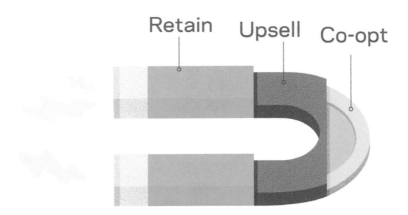

A quick and dirty way to do this is to encourage donors to share the fact they donated on their social media. All you need is a little nudge and a link at the end of the donation process or in the 'thank you' email.

The next step, for you

So you know the steps that your users are going to take. But what about you? The ability to think about your users' needs and put them first is a skill you'll need to develop. If you're unable to empathise with those who support you then they're going to struggle to empathise with you.

If you know your supporters though, you'll be able to make donating easy for them, you'll be able to deepen your relationship with them, and you'll even be able to find others just like them, which is what the next chapter is all about.

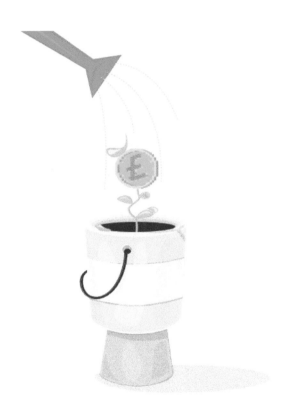

Chapter 4

Grow a digital audience

Overview

When you want people to give money to you, in the middle of a busy city or town centre, your fundraising team can see your audience right in front of them. And while it's not always easy to catch their attention, and they may go some way to avoid the smiley people with clipboards (ever noticed how everyone is mysteriously on their phones when they walk past a charity chugger?), at least you know that they are there.

Admittedly, digital audiences are a little harder to see. Unless you count a sea of avatars on a social media feed, or a list of emails on your mailing list.

The thing with digital is that your relationship can be pretty one-sided. You can find your audiences, sure. But if you want to catch their eye, you're going to have to work at it.

It's all about relationships

People often have to see something online multiple times before they finally engage or sign-up. It's true:

- 40% of eCommerce transactions are carried out more than 24 hours after a user's first visit to the website.

- 60% of revenue is attributable to customers who don't buy on their first visit.[22]

It's a lot like dating, when you think about it. You have to work on relationships, you can't just give a swift hello and expect the other party to do all of the work.

When it comes to reaching new and existing audiences here are the channels that should matter to you, and the best ways to use them.

Your website

We couldn't start without mentioning the most obvious digital channel – your website. If you're reading this, hopefully you already have one.

The audience for your website is likely to be a mix of different demographics, with a skew towards service users and their families, volunteers and supporters.

If someone is on your website, it's likely that they already have some form of relationship with you, even if it's early days. So this is good potential traffic for digital fundraising. They're already warm to your message.

Your website should have a general 'donate now' page, with links to a digital giving platform or a payment gateway form, which is an obvious start.

But pages about your campaigns, and other ways to give – such as lotteries, legacy giving, corporate support – should also be on the site in a 'Get Involved' or 'Support Us' section.

Perhaps more integral to your website than any of these things though, is your content. And that might seem controversial, but, in order for you to get anything from your supporters, you're going to want to be giving them something in return.

Think about why people are on your website in the first place. Did they come looking for advice? Are they after key information that only you can provide? Have you services that could change their lives?

In order to get people to your website in the first place, you need to make sure that your content is up-to-scratch. People don't always visit a charity website with the sole purpose of donating – what a fine thing that would be if they did.

Many people will arrive on pages of your site (such as service pages, news and blog posts, and advice) either through search engines or a link from another channel, if you're providing the information that they need. So consider the routes your users are taking and make sure you push your campaigns and donation pages throughout your site. You may wish to promote your fundraising campaign in a prominent place on the homepage too, but remember that not everyone will enter your site through the homepage.

Your website should have regular and relevant calls to action on all relevant pages too. For example, on your services page – do you let people know that these services are made possible by donations and link to your donate now page? Do you utilise sidebar content, or think about how you can cross-link content when you're producing it? Have you considered the importance of microcopy (the little bits of text on buttons and headings all over your site) and messaging? And what about investing some time into user journeys – trying to assess how your users might use your site now, and whether you could improve on this?

You can boost traffic by considering all of these points, as well as regularly updating your website with the kind of content that will interest your target audiences. Ultimately, if your content matches up with what people are searching for, then it will be found, and if it's interesting enough, it will also be shared on social media and emailed to friends.

If you don't have time to write this content, consider investing in someone who can. The importance of content is often overlooked and left until last, which is a bit like falling at the last hurdle when websites are concerned.

Don't underestimate the power of good content.

Your newsletter

Whilst you can influence how many people arrive at your website, dictating how your audience interacts with you is often harder. However, this is where newsletters shine.

A user doesn't have to proactively seek you out, or even think about you; you get to remind them about your existence – and your brilliant new campaign – whenever you want.

Email provides a great return-on-investment for charity fundraisers, with one third of all overall digital fundraising revenue generated as a result of email[11]. In 2015, every £1 that businesses spent on email created £38 in return. Although this figure is for business-oriented emails, this level of success is very achievable within the charity sector, and we often see higher.

If you don't have a mailing list, or you do but never use it, you really need to start building one. You technically can do this by asking for permission every time you get someone's email address. But, ideally, you also want a subscription form on your website to collect email addresses passively whilst you do other things.

Once you have a mailing list in place, there are a few rules you should follow:

- Don't make the mistake of only emailing when you want something.

- Aim for a newsletter once every three to nine weeks. That's not often enough to annoy, but frequent enough to remind people they signed up in the first place. It will also keep the relationship warm for when you do ask for a donation. Currently, 15% of nonprofits send out emails at least weekly, and 74% email at least monthly[23].

- As for send time, sending an email between 2pm and 5pm on a weekday is the usually the best time to send overall.[24].

However, if everyone followed this trend (which doesn't just apply to charities), it could be that this time period becomes oversaturated and less effective. Test with your own audiences at different times to see what works.

- Don't call your newsletter a 'newsletter' in the subject line. Keep the subject line descriptive, but make people **want** to open it.

- Keep the content punchy: don't waste time "welcoming" people with an opening statement. Most people are impatient when put in front of an email inbox, so get to the point.

- Make the content of the newsletter **interesting or useful** to your audience. Don't just think about what you want to shout out at them.

- Include one or more asks that link to your campaign or donation pages.

- Segment your email list by either asking, or manually recording, a category for each subscriber. When you come to compose an email you can either just email people in a particular segment, or even swap words or content based on the type of person receiving the email. On average a segmented newsletter gets 52% more clicks than a non segmented one.

MailChimp (http://www.mailchimp.com) is the recommended platform for managing your emails. It's easy-to-use and deals with a lot of the fiddly details for you; such as double-opting-in users by confirming their sign-up with an email, and automatically dealing with unsubscription requests. Plus, it's free to use if you have less than 2,000 subscribers.

As well as the main website, MailChimp also offers MailChimp Snap (http://mailchimp.com/features/mailchimp-snap/) – an app which enables you to create newsletters, simply and quickly, from your mobile device.

As well as being easy to use, MailChimp Snap would be a useful campaign tool for more visual projects. For example, sending daily email updates to your subscribers, showing the work you have done that day. That might be meeting some of your service-users and sharing their story, or showing the physical work your team have done while building a new school in an area that needs it. Think of it as the love-child of email and Instagram – visual updates, with a more guaranteed reach.

Your social media

Social media can work for fundraising. More than half of the traffic to JustGiving now comes from Facebook[25], whilst every share of a JustGiving campaign to Facebook is worth, on average, an additional £4.50 in donations.

The average JustGiving donation originating from Facebook is £19. The equivalent figures for Twitter are £1.80 and £22 respectively.[26]

*2014 experienced a drop due to the Ice Bucket Challenge. The average donation for this campaign was much smaller at £16.11[28], bringing the overall average donation through social media down.

Average JustGiving donation through social media.[27]

Using social media to fundraise can be difficult at first. Knowing what to share, and when to share it comes with practice. There are many social media campaigns that have underperformed, not because they were terrible, but because they failed to understand their audience. Let's take a look at one, and see how, with just a few tweaks, it could have been a success.

This is what Save Doncaster Libraries tried when using social media to raise funds. Do you think this works?

Save Don Libs @doncasterlibs 25 Feb

help us fund our judicial review - URGENTLY - we need to match Legal Aid. Send paypal donations from your paypal to johnshep50@talktalk.net

If you're curious enough to click a link, you'll find a blog post that is not much better. There's quite a lot of begging for donations, then a moan about a local councillor – none of it inspires a reader to find a reason to give. But if you do get to the end, there's a photograph of an eight year-old girl holding a little drawing about what her library means to her.

A young Doncaster Libraries supporter.

The image is attention-grabbing, powerful, emotive and authentic. It's great content. It's your reason to pay attention, to share; your reason to give.

Imagine if they'd posted that on social media, then linked to a page about it, with more information about their cause and an appeal for donations. We can guarantee the response would have been much better.

Play to the strengths of your platform

Facebook

Facebook essentially works with a newsfeed. It's made up of content from people you choose to befriend, and companies and organisations you like (with a few ads thrown in). It seems simple – get people to like your page, and then you'll be able to reach them whenever you like, right?

Wrong. Let's talk about the Facebook's News Feed Algorithm – an artificial intelligence that filters out posts from friends and pages that you don't read or interact with much. This means if you keep asking people for money, or sharing stuff other people aren't interested in, then Facebook is gradually showing your posts in fewer and fewer people's feeds.

If you monitor the content you're sharing, you're more likely to get some interaction and you're more likely to be seen. Why? Facebook will prioritise content that shows regular interaction so, if you pay attention to what works and what doesn't, you can soon work out how to nudge yourself up in the newsfeed game.

On the flip-side, you can conveniently pay to override this algorithm by 'promoting a post', which we talk about more on page 81.

On Facebook, ensure you use your personal Facebook account to set up a Page for your organisation. You'll then be the 'Admin' of this page and you'll be able to access it through your personal account. Facebook may ban you if you set up an individual page pretending to be an organisation, as it requires all personal accounts to be for

Example: The Cheque Mistakes

A bad (left) and good (right) example of a Facebook post.

Lots of us share out-of-context pictures of older people holding cheques. It doesn't work. What actually works are emotive images and stories that show the power of your work and the difference your supporters can make by supporting you. Here's what actually works. It's not just about posting though. Start and join conversations – don't just push your messages out. The clue is in the name **social** media.

On social media, when people share or interact, it will alert **their** friends and followers, and some will check you out and like, follow, or even subscribe.

a real person with a real name, and you could quickly lose all of the relationships and interaction you've gained if Facebook cottons on, especially now that users can report misuse.

Twitter

Twitter is great at introducing you to new people from around the world, but you can make it work locally for you too. Use the search feature and enter local places, landmarks, football teams, and towns. This will show you people talking about local issues, who you can then follow or interact with to make them aware of you. Many will follow back. Quite often these might be local journalists, councillors, MPs, minor celebrities; all useful people to be communicating with.

On Twitter, register an account like any other. Set your name to be the name of your organisation, and your profile image to be your logo. Ensure your location is set correctly and your biography contains keywords, and even hashtags, to make you easy to find. Pay a little attention to your Twitter page – details like matching your theme to your brand colours makes you look that little bit more official.

YouTube

Video is a powerful fundraising tool with the ability to communicate an emotional message effectively. Research on crowdfunding has shown that, all else being equal, a crowdfunding campaign has a 35% higher chance of success if a video is included[29]. And a study that looked at the reasons for participating in charitable actions (donating, volunteering, event attendance, contacting MP, etc) showed that 41% of people watched an online video, which led them to act.[30]

Video takes more work to put together, but for a mildly tech-savvy individual it's actually very accessible. Nowadays, you can create good quality video content with just a smartphone and a bit of thought.

When it comes to video, YouTube is the place to be, with over 1 billion active users[31]. It's accessible on a range of devices, in 61 languages and is being used in 75 countries.

While technically, YouTube is a social media network, it's unlikely you'll have many subscribers, so it's most useful as a place to host videos to cross-promote on other channels and embed on your web pages.

It also helps with SEO. Google acquired YouTube in 2006, mainly due to its overwhelming influential search and social presence. Used together, the two platforms can provide you with a marketing boost, because YouTube videos are ranked routinely high on Google search pages.

So, while you might have been hoping to be charity's next Zoella, being a YouTube sensation shouldn't be your sole priority. There are even more benefits:

- Audiences are about 10 times more likely to engage, embed, share, and comment on video content, than blogs or other related social posts.[32]

- Videos increase people's understanding of your product or service by 74%.[33]

- Using videos on landing pages increases conversions by 86%.[34]

YouTube isn't a platform you're likely to use as regularly as Facebook or Twitter, so we won't touch on it too much more in the rest of this book. But we do have some tips you should be following when you decide to make the most of what it can offer.

1. YouTube recommends that you add a thumbnail to every video you upload to increase the chances of people choosing your video in a list of search results. It suggests that your thumbnails:

   • have a resolution of 1280x720 (with a minimum width of 640 pixels)

   • are uploaded in image formats such as .JPG, .GIF, .BMP, or .PNG

   • remain under the 2 MB limit

   • use a 16:9 aspect ratio as it's the most used in YouTube players and previews

2. Don't forget to add appropriate tags to your videos. Not only will this help them come up in related searches, it also helps your other videos become more discoverable. If you consistently use a tag that is unique to all of your videos, then when one of your videos is playing, your other videos will show in the sidebar and end slate, encouraging viewers and to click and watch another.

3. When it comes to titles, think about that 'click-bait' element, but also what is likely to be searched for, so you'll be found in the right YouTube and Google searches. If you aren't sure what to choose, think about the kind of search term you would like to be found under and go from there.

4. Make sure you sign up for YouTube's Nonprofit Programme, as this will allow you to make parts of the video clickable straight to your campaign or donation page at that crucial moment.

5. And finally, following on from the point above, don't forget to add those calls to action on your videos, just like you would with any other content. Pay attention to clickable hot spots and your description box too. It's always useful to have a quick bio and related links for each video you create. Give your viewers a place to go next.

What about the rest?

Facebook, Twitter and YouTube are the big three social networks, the ones which nearly every charity should be using. There are many, many more though; like Pinterest, Instagram, LinkedIn and Google+, all of which offer something unique. Of a study done in the U.S., 98% of charities and nonprofits are active on at least one social media site, with YouTube (97%), Facebook (92%) and Twitter (86%) most favoured.

Pinterest (72%) and LinkedIn (57%) were also found to be popular in the study, and, three times as many charities use newcomer photo app, Snapchat (9%), as they do Tumblr (3%).[35]

Experiment with ones that fit your charity. If you have a lot of great photo opportunities then perhaps check out Instagram and Pinterest. If you're more focused on getting funding from businesses then LinkedIn may prove fruitful for you.

But make sure you don't sign up to so many channels you can't be good. You'll make more digital funds if you excel on one platform, rather than be mediocre on many.

Other people's channels

Much like real-life, building relationships online is a gradual, long-term process. Especially with multiple people in the mix. And multiple conversations happening all at once.

It takes time, and it's certainly not easy. You consistently need to be useful and interesting in order to build up the audience for your website, your social media, or your newsletter.

Or you can cheat, and pay for exposure, but this makes it difficult to make a return.

There is a third way though. Why spend lots of resources on building up your own channels to push your campaign, when you may have supporters who have already done all the hard work?

Let's say this is you on Twitter, a tiny bird in this vast grey empty space. Talking about your campaign to no one, which is what it feels like sometimes.

In this world, your voice is quiet, almost a whisper. But even a whisper can be powerful if it's into the right ear. Like the ear of someone very good at Twitter, someone with lots of people following them and hanging off their every word. They can turn your whisper into a shout.

Not only will this mean you instantly reach far more people, but these supporters will also phrase your campaign in a way that appeals to their audience far better than you could.

These people are known as your influencers. You need to keep an eye out for them on social media. Influencers might be celebrities who have a link to your cause, they might run big websites, or write popular blogs about topics such as parenting, disability, food, and fashion.

Focusing your limited time and resources on building relationships with these people so they want to share your messages is a great strategy.

Example: Team Honk

If you're dubious as to whether influencers could work for you, here's a brilliant example of their power and, maybe more impressively, their dedication.

Team Honk was born in 2012, when three parenting bloggers, Annie Spratt, Tanya Barrow and Penny Alexander, approached Comic Relief to launch some blogger fundraising.

The Team Honk Bloggers.

Why? Well, we asked Tanya: "Well, as bloggers we have a voice. Be that for ranting about the Kardashians being all over the Daily Mail again. Or for talking about a brand we love. Or, we can use that voice to reach out our readers, to our communities and get their support.

"We used our blogs to come together to raise awareness for Comic Relief; publishing their content, and creating our own from trips with them to Africa. And we fundraised. But we brought the blog community together to do that, and what I loved was seeing new friendships come from that with bloggers that were local to each other and had never met. Empowering people who knew they had made a difference was incredible and life-changing for me, and made me want to do more."

Which is why, something that was born from a simple ask in 2012, has led to the biggest charity parent blogging campaign so far, with over 250 posts written and linked up to the Team Honk website. Team Honk have gone on to fundraise every year, with a UK-wide relay, and a danceathon. The team have gained the support of Jonathan Ross and Davina McCall. And, in the three years since Team Honk began, the hard work and dedication of three bloggers, and their community, has raised almost £70,000 for Comic Relief.

Traditional media

Even though we're fundraising digitally, traditional media can still play a significant part in driving interest to your campaign. Don't overlook it.

Don't be afraid to ask national and local journalists, radio stations and even TV broadcasters for coverage of your digital fundraising campaign. These outlets will likely have a popular website and social media feeds, which could provide you with a huge boost in traffic.

Don't be frightened to play the charity card. Remember that these news outlets need stories, and you have engaging, moving, life-changing stories by the bucketload, about things that really matter to people in your community.

Most local outlets write stories that use individuals to talk about broader subjects. For instance, it's unlikely that a local paper will dedicate a page to fighting a specific illness, but they would cover the personal battle of a local individual, in the form of a case study. Provide this for them and make their job easy.

Crucially, to make it work best for your digital campaign, make sure you ask for a link on their website. Why? This process is called link building, and, in short, it's the process of getting your links on other successful websites. This will help to further boost your rankings in search engines, which means you're likely to be presented to more potential supporters.

Also: a final word of advice, share the story on your social channels. Mention them, and they will probably re-share or retweet on their channel, for an extra boost.

Example: Manchester Dogs' Home

Take Manchester Dogs' Home. They got a windfall after massive support on social media when an arsonist burnt down their facility, killing 60 dogs in the process.

Support was pushed over the tipping point by the Manchester Evening News, who set up the JustGiving page and pushed it mercilessly on their website, social media and in their newspaper.

In the end, they managed to raise £1.4 million in a matter of days, which included donations from Simon Cowell and Mario Balotelli. The money has gone towards a new, temporary adoption centre, with plans for a permanent facility already in place.

Paid advertisement

If all this sounds like a bit too much work, or you can't get the size of audience you need any other way, you can pay for exposure online with ads. Adverts allow you to reach people who wouldn't otherwise see your content. They allow your content to be displayed more prominently, whether that's through search results, social media or websites. Ads can consist of text, images, videos, or a mix.

Buying ads

You can buy ads on Facebook, Twitter, YouTube, Google (and other search engines) and on some websites too.

You can pay to have these ads visible in a variety of ways:

- Ad impressions: paying for a certain number of people to view them.

- Cost-per-click: paying every time someone clicks on an ad.

- Conversions: Facebook also lets you pay for 'conversions', although this is more expensive.

The cost of advertising varies depending on the website you're using and the types of people you'e targeting the ad to. Social networks and search sites let you 'bid' and will tell you how much the traffic would be worth to you. The more you bid, the more people see your ad.

Ads on websites and search engines always push people towards a web page. Ads on social media can either push people to a webpage, a social media account, or a piece of content like a YouTube video or Facebook post.

Getting the best results

So how can you ensure that you get the best from your advertising? Here we have a few examples, and some best-practice guidance too.

Search Engine

Search engine ads work best if you can give someone something they might be looking for. And by that, we mean, think of why your supporters might be using search engines, and, perhaps more importantly, which search results you want to appear within.

This is currently a trick that is missed by many in the charity sector.

An example of Google search results listing.

UK charities spend just 2% of their annual advertising budget on online ads (up from 1% in 2006). In comparison, the rest of the advertising industry has seen online advertising grow from 17% in 2006 to over 46% now.[36]

The best thing you can do with search engine advertisements, is to make sure you have the right sort of content that matches the search term you are investing in. So if you want to really make the most of coming up-top for a search about "depression advice" or "volunteering in Manchester", then make sure you have the content they are looking for, so your new visitors don't just visit and leave in disappointment.

Social

Social ads work best if you can give someone something fun, social or a way to pass time. That is, after all, why we use social media.

While keeping it fun and interesting is a useful piece of advice for any social channel, there are some specific things you can do depending on which channel you are using.

Facebook

Facebook has a type of advertising called a Promoted Post which is a great way to reach current and new audiences now that Facebook has made organic reach more challenging.

A promoted Facebook post from Colour Run UK.

A side benefit of this is that it allows you to target the post to specific people, something that organic content doesn't do.

You can create a Promoted Post, which you can think of as a dedicated advert, or you can opt to boost a post that you have already published.

Just ensure that you:

- Promote or boost a post that is likely to resonate with your audience. Don't promote a general update, or spend all of your budget on promoting fundraising asks.

- Remember to stay fun and interesting. Each promoted post is a chance to get views and likes and comments and shares; it's a chance to engage those people so you show up in their feed again. If you only promote selfish asks then people won't do this, and your money won't be well spent.

- Take note of the analytics Facebook provides you with. If you don't get a great response to a post first time around, don't promote it in a bid to get the interaction that you want. If a post isn't right, it won't get much interaction, whether you pay or not.

- Consider the 20% text within images rule. If your post includes an image, which also features text, it won't be approved by Facebook unless the image is made up of less than 20% text. You can use Facebook's Grid Tool (https://www.facebook.com/ads/tools/text_overlay) to help you check each image before you post.

- Promote content that benefits your audience and give them more reason to follow you. It may sound simple, but giveaways, useful updates or tools are far more likely to encourage people to stick around.

Twitter

Twitter ads follow a similar format to Facebook ads, in that you can promote a tweet to a targeted audience on a pay per click basis.

You can set up Twitter ads to achieve certain objectives. Options include: tweet engagements, website clicks and conversions, app installs or app re-engagements, video views, followers and leads.

You can also set up a custom campaign, if you don't want your ads to be objective-based.

When creating your ads for Twitter, consider how you can attract people to your ad quickly, as people will only briefly see the ad in your timeline. Try using images to grab people's attention, and think of the hashtags that are relevant too.

As with Facebook, make sure you are promoting content that your followers want to see. Don't promote content that has failed before; pay attention to the analytics that Twitter provides you with and learn from them.

Targeting

Now we know the methods we can use, what about who we aim our adverts at?

Targeting is a feature of search and social media advertising that is very powerful for fundraisers. You can advertise to people in a particular place, a certain age-group, or even people with an interest in a certain subject, so you're not wasting money on views or clicks from people outside your target audience.

For search, you generally target based on what people are searching for, and the terms you want to appear above or beside.

On social, you can specify age ranges, genders, marital statuses; even interests.

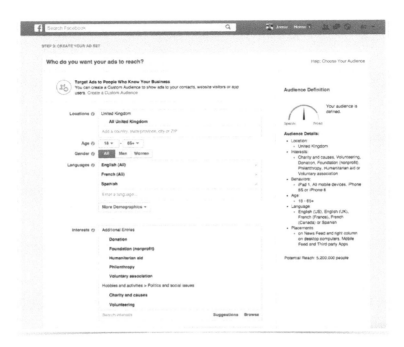

Choosing the audience target with Facebook ads.

Many people try a small spend on social media ads. Then if it doesn't work well immediately, they stop and write it off. That's not the best way to go.

A better way to work is to set up a handful of ads with different messages, images and target audiences. See which works the best, ditch the ones that don't, and increase the amount that you're spending on the ones that are delivering the best results

Budgets & Bids

Setting budgets allows you to control your level of spend, and also control how prominent your ads are.

Budgets are usually set overall, or daily. Bids are the maximum you will pay for ad space or per click. The more demand there is for a particular space, or audience target, the higher you'll need to bid.

Earlier in the book, on page 24, we talked about Return on Investment (ROI). If you know how much money you're making from each visitor to your campaign page, you know what the maximum you can spend on ads is.

For example

- 10,000 visits to your campaign page (visits).

- 250 donations to your campaign (a 2.5% conversion rate).

- £30 average donation.

- So: £30 x 250 = £7,500 in income

- £7,500 / 10,000 visits = £0.75 on average per visitor.

- Average donation x number of donations/visits to get that donation = income of 75p per visitor.

- Therefore, the maximum you should bid on ads: 70p, to make a 5p profit.

$$\frac{£30 \text{ (average donation)} \times 250 \text{ (number of donations)}}{10,000 \text{ (visits to get that donation)}}$$

= £0.75

on average per visitor

If you don't want to spend anything, but you're okay with paperwork, Google offers charities free advertisements with something called Google AdWords Grants. You can get up to $12,500 of free ads, but the catch is you can't compete with 'commercial' search terms, and you can't bid more than $2.00 per ad, which limits your ability to show up for very popular searches. However, if you have the time and creativity, lots of less popular searches can add up to the level of traffic from one popular search term.

Techniques you should be using

So, we've identified the ways in which we can reach our audiences. But it's not just about doing these things – it's about doing them well.

Regardless of how you're using digital, there are plenty of things that you can try if you want to get results. One of the most important things we can teach you is the importance of consistency – so make sure you consider all of these points and apply them to whatever you do. They work – trust us.

Remember relationships

Fundraising is all about relationships, and digital is no different. It isn't just a collection of platforms from which you can talk at people; it's a way to talk to people. You talk to people all the time, day-to-day. You just need to do this online too. It's not a scary new skill reserved for the next generation, it's just a bit harder to do it when the person isn't stood in front of you.

If you look at what you're about to to share and imagine saying it to someone's face, it might make you think twice about asking again for donations, or the way you phrase things.

Be useful and interesting

Your content doesn't have to be big, amazing, or even particularly impressive. It just needs to be one of two things: useful or interesting.

Think about the things you click on or interact with, and remember that your audience will have their own preferences too. Relationship-building is often about asking questions, showing an interest, and showing that you like and value similar things. You wouldn't talk about yourself all day, and the same applies online.

Try to model yourselves on the persona of a brainy friend. Your charity knows a lot about something that a lot of people, and potential donors, care about. Use this as an opportunity to engage with them.

Write blog posts that share interesting updates around your cause, or are topical, not just introducing your latest member of staff. Refresh your website content so that it's inviting and useful. Think about how donors might find you - what would they search for? What would you like to show up in search results for? You'll never show up if you don't find the answers to your audience's questions.

Think about how you can help your users, so they will, in turn, help you.

Mix-up your content

Variety is the spice of life. It's good to remember that content can come in many different forms.

Not only is this more varied for your audience, and more interesting, but it can help you to make the most of social channels too. A video of your work may bring it to life, and reach a new audience on YouTube. An infographic is shareable, memorable and a really quick way of sharing content.

And even then, you can mix up your content by using links, quotes, lists and real imagery, instead of just text and a standard stock image.

Facebook also seems to be more willing to show your posts to a wider audience if you vary your posts. And what if you were the first charity to really make good use of Periscope, or Snapchat?

Be creative - we all like to see something different.

Think mobile

Consumers are now nearly twice as likely to share content on social networks through mobile devices compared to desktop (7.7% vs 4.1%)[37]. And, if that wasn't enough to convince you, take a look at this comparison study[38], that looks at the share of time spent with selected categories of online content, between mobile and desktop

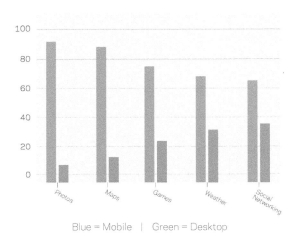

Blue = Mobile | Green = Desktop

So you need to be considering whether or not your content is accessible by mobiles.

It's not just about getting the tweet-length right – consider where you are sending your followers afterwards. Is your site responsive? Is that form tricky to fill in? If so, fix it.

Get visual

As the saying goes: "A picture paints a thousand words." Images can tell your audience a lot of things in a short space of time. They can bring things to life. And they are also much more universally understood, and faster to process. If you need convincing – think of how much quicker it is to draw a circle than describe it.

Images are now out-performing videos because they are easy-to-view on a mobile screen. Mobiles are the device of choice for looking at pictures – 92% of photo viewing is now done through phones and tablets[39]. So if you want to attract attention, get visual.

Research has also shown that tweets with photos get 313% more engagement[40] than those without, but use them sensibly as no one likes a same-old, same-old timeline.

Ask nicely

When it comes to the ask, don't just ask. And don't ask too often. If you go back to real-life for a moment, no one likes the friend who always asks to 'borrow' things and then disappears when you need them back. In the same way, your charity shouldn't just ask for donations and then let your supporters down by not providing useful content, valuable services, relationships and support. Be a giver, not just a taker.

Share interesting things, shocking facts, moving images and quotes. Only one in five voluntary sector organisations is regularly sharing image and video content through social media[41], so this is an area to improve. Why? Do these things so people want to listen to what you have to say, and find you interesting. Then, if you have a campaign that relates to the things you're sharing, link them together.

Whilst direct donations can work, the best campaign mechanics on social media tend to be things that help people meet people, have fun, or be social (funny that). That's why they're on social media, after all. Things like competitions, lotteries and fundraising events all work well, as they offer either a sense of excitement or community.

You've found them – now what?

Once you've hunted down your audience, and gained their trust, do they just donate and do the rest for you?

Absolutely not. Nice thought though.

As the saying goes: "You can lead a horse to water, but you can't make it drink." You can lead a potential donor to your website, but you can't make them give.

Unless you're persuasive...

Chapter 5

Persuade them to give

Overview

So what magic words do we need to say online to get someone to give?

Sadly, it's not that easy. This isn't a lesson at Hogwarts. This is the real world and there's no combination of words that will convince everyone to give - every audience, every cause and every channel responds in a different way. That's why trying things out on your own audiences and measuring what works is the only way to go.

And while there aren't any magic words, there's still an element of wizardry involved in the form of insight, messaging and strategy. There are things you can do to persuade people to give that tend to work well across campaigns and, at the very least, will get you thinking about persuading instead of just asking.

Choose your voice

The person asking for donations is a big factor in persuasion. If it's someone with an authentic, trustworthy voice, who has no agenda, then it will magnify the impact of the message.

That means video messages from service users and happy donors may be more powerful than a statement from the Head of Fundraising or Chief Executive.

27% of the public still give a rating of between 0-5 out of 10 for their trust and confidence in charities. And, almost three in five (59%) believe charities spend too much on salaries and administration[42]. So think about these problem areas and think of ways you can combat them.

Another point to remember is that there's no one more influential than friends and family. In fact, 65% of people who support a charity online report that they first heard about the cause from a family member or friend on social media. And 75% of people report that they feel that they have influence over friends and family.[43]

In the next chapter, we'll look at how to use this fact to boost your digital fundraising whilst reducing the work you have to put in... Now, that's **almost** magic.

Grab attention

People have to notice you and your campaign before they can be persuaded.

Make sure you're using the channels that reach your target audiences and prioritise being interesting and attention-grabbing. How you achieve this depends on the channel you're using, and the audience you're appealing to.

In general, images of people work best to capture initial interest, so make sure you're capturing them. From a psychological perspective, a study has found that the presence of 'real people' and images of eyes have a significant positive effect on donations. Why? Because, as humans, we are fine-tuned to react to the presence of others, which is all part of conforming to society'.[44]

Tailor your message

You might know what you want to say, but there's a big difference in the ways that you can say it.

Only 32% of charities are using information about a supporter's interests within their communications. Could it be that we're all making the mistake of talking about ourselves too much?[45]

* 74% of online consumers get frustrated with websites when content (e.g. offers, ads, and promotions) appear to have nothing to do with their interests. And there's no reason why this won't apply to charity websites too.[46]

So, are you considering different audience types every time you update? Have you considered men, women, children, the older generation? Think about your audience groups and what might best speak to them.

Here at Reason Digital, we recently conducted research into the charitable attitudes and behaviours of 16-24 year olds (http://reasondigital.com/advice-and-training/research-young-people-charity-a-paper/).

We found that these millennials, unsurprisingly, faced greater financial barriers to donating than the UK average. This is reflected in less-frequent and lower-value donations, but a stronger intention to be donating more in 10 years' time. However, there was also a higher degree of apathy, disinterest and distrust of charities among young adults compared to the rest of society.[47]

As a result, it would be wise to segment your audience on the basis of age, and reduce what is being asked of younger viewers/recipients/stakeholders. Rather, it might be a wise campaign strategy to focus your efforts on building long-term relationships and the possibility of non-monetary involvement (volunteering and event attendance, for example) from 16-24 year olds, and targeting donation asks at those aged 25+.

If you try a one-size-fits all approach, chances are you're going to end up with something that will fit no-one.

You also need to make sure that you aren't just sharing the same message over and over again. While you can't expect 100% of your followers to see 100% of your updates, chances are a few will pick-up on lazy tweets if you don't mix things up now and again. Repetitive messaging looks like spam, and no one likes that.

It's also worth making a note of what type of messaging works best and repeating that style. That might be a chatty update, a case study, a shocking stat, or a powerful quote. Pay attention to interaction and repeat what works.

Show off your supporters

In our online world the constant flood of information, messages, emails and distractions can be stressful. It almost makes you pine for simpler times, back when there were only two channels on TV, phones were used for speaking, and the only way to write to people was in a letter. A lot has changed since then though; the internet has changed how people communicate, how people consume, and even the way people think.[48] [49] [50]

Making decisions under stress makes people rely on 'heuristics', which is a posh term for 'mental shortcuts based on experience'. These are little tricks the mind takes to avoid having to do any heavy thinking, and the most powerful one of all is called social proof.

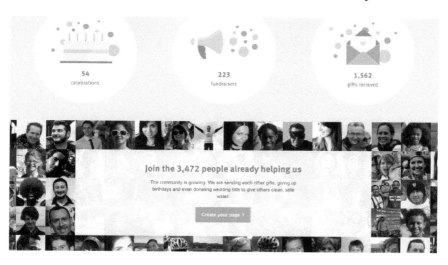

Wahoo from Water aid uses stats about engagement to encourage new registrations.

Social proof controls the outcome of many of the decisions you have to make, especially if you're in a hurry. Rather than think through all the pros and cons of something, you can just look and see what most other people are doing and do that. Imagine visiting a new city and trying to find the best place to eat. When you're hungry you're not going to thoroughly research every restaurant in the area, instead you'll think to yourself: "That place looks nice, plus it's busy, so it must be good." We assume that if something is popular, then there must be a reason for it.

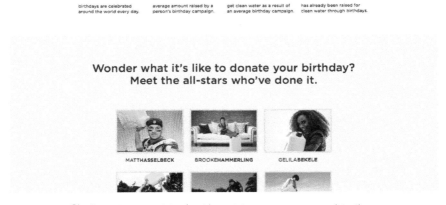

Charity: water uses stats about impact to encourage new registrations.

Restaurants have it easy; people can peer through a window to check how busy a restaurant is. With charities though, you have put a bit more effort in. So how can you put your supporters in your front window?

Appeal to emotions

People choose to give with their heart, not their head. The more you use things that appeal to our more rational side – like statistics – the more likely someone is to have their emotional journey to donation derailed by analytical thinking.

This is why successful lotteries appeal to players' sense of fun, uncertainty and not-knowingness, rather than rationality, in convincing them to play more. And this concept isn't anything new – it's been the case since history began. As humans, we never evolved to the point where we could comprehend subtle differences in numbers.[51]

For example, we can visualise one thing, or ten things thanks to our fingers or toes, and we can even visualise 100, if we think of a large crowd of people. But if we try and visualise a million things, our ability fails.

Put more simply, Mother Teresa once said: "If I look at the mass, I will never act. If I look at the one, I will."

So, by the same logic, charities should not appeal too much to the rationality of donors; donations are always important, but they are often mired in complexity, admin, everyday expenditure and not-very-glamorous necessities. This 'real-world' quantification of impact will not encourage anybody to act, so appeal instead to the emotional cues which invoke sympathy, empathy, compassion or passion in your stakeholders.

On that note, making the issue that you are tackling real for people should be your priority. So how do we do that? By using emotionally appealing content and stories. 56% of those that support nonprofits on social media confirm that compelling storytelling is what motivates them to take action.

To make the most of these stories, you should ideally identify that moment when the emotion is at its strongest, then follow it with an ask. This is when people are most likely to give.

Research on viral videos shows that the emotion can be anything. The fact there is emotion, and it has a moment of intensity in your content, is what's key to pushing someone over into taking action.

This idea isn't new, but it's particularly powerful in digital fundraising.

Stories vs. Stats

In 2006, researchers studied what prompts resulted in the highest return of donations to a Save the Children campaign. They tested how much out of an available $5 limit each participant donated to the cause on the basis of whether the beneficiary of the donation was 'identifiable' (the personal story of a young girl named Rokia) or 'statistical' (a general statistic about how many people need help).

A Day in the Life in Mali with Rokia

Rokia is a bright eight-year-old girl who lives in the western African nation of Mali. She lives with her parents and five siblings on a small subsistence farm.

When Save the Children first started working in her village, Rokia's family was barely scraping by on their crops of corn, potatoes, sorghum and peanuts. They are one of the lucky families, as they have a few mango trees, which helps to supplement their low income and provides much needed food for the family.

Rokia was among the first participants in our sponsorship-funded program and she benefits from our Basic Education and School Health and Nutrition work. Here she is pictured with her mother.

Rokia was among the first participants in Save the Children's sponsorship-funded program in her village. Since 2009, Rokia has benefitted from our education, health and nutrition programs. Each year Save the Children provides vitamin A, iron, and deworming treatment to improve Rokia's health.

Rokia leads an active life. "I like to keep busy with my family and friends," Rokia says with a smile, happy to split her time between school, play and chores.

A big part of Rokia's busy day is doing whatever she can to help her family. She gets up early to get ready for school and do chores while it is still cool — temperatures often top 100 degrees by midday.

'Identifiable' story of Rokia, from a Save the Children campaign.

Interestingly, they found that, whilst identifiable victims generated the highest average donation, the value of this was almost halved when participants were encouraged to think analytically beforehand (about entirely unrelated things!).[54]

Put the donor's needs first

Charity is often thought of as a selfless act, but we need to find ways to make it work for the donor, as well as us, and stress these in our messaging if we want to persuade more people to give.

Common ineffective messages include:

> *"We need to raise £10,000 a month to continue to exist."*

> *"We rely on the help of generous donors to operate our services."*

> *"Become one of our supporters today."*

You might get away with these messages in direct mail but, in the digital world, they just won't work. It's much better to focus on the donor's needs and feelings. They don't want to sustain your organisation; they want to make a difference, change a life, make a stand. You're giving them the way to do it. Don't undersell that.

And while you're at it, don't make your donors' contributions feel like a drop in a very vast ocean by banging on about your fundraising target.

Show your impact

Charity is about people helping others. Most people agree that charities do good, but that feeling is often tempered by skepticism and distrust. Nearly everyone who supports charities believes they should be told by charities how their donations are spent (96%), and what helps those affected (94%). So give the people what they want. Be transparent and show your impact.

Be careful of how you do this though; make sure you say it in an appropriate voice. Research has shown that placing too much emphasis upon the scientific way that you've calculated impact can actually be a deterrent to some people donating. Speak like normal people, not stat-spouting robots – be reassuring, prove you make a difference, and tell a story. Don't bore your reader, nor dissuade them with over-scientific, dehumanising explanations of the minutiae of donations.

Make it seem achievable

Most donors want to make a difference. That means to persuade them to give you must do two key things:

- Show them how giving to you will have an impact.

- Show them that what is a significant amount of money to them, is not an insignificant sum of money when it comes to making a difference.

Breaking down your mission into smaller pieces is how you achieve this second point. Don't say you want to eliminate late-life loneliness for ever – say you want to do it for 20 people at Christmas. Put a totaliser alongside it, to show what a massive contribution £50 would be to that goal.

Also, we know that focusing on the huge amount you need to raise can make donors feel like their contribution would be insignificant and give them an excuse not to go ahead. So don't try to shock them with how much money you need to operate per day. Focus on the difference that they can make by supporting you.

Show a sense of urgency

If someone's looking at some digital communications from you, then they're likely just a click away from something that feels more urgent or more fun. Be it an email from their boss, or a video of a cat falling off a bed. Digital is very distracting.

This is why bringing a sense of urgency is key. Make them feel they have to do it now - that they can't put it off until tomorrow - and you'll find your messages convert many more people.

There are two ways to do this:

One way is to focus on a sense of crisis, or on the cause. Give supporters a sense of urgency. That might be the chance to help eliminate something before a deadline, or tackle something that threatens to get so bad it might start hurting or killing people. Alternatively, the ability to help someone before a generally recognised milestone/time - like the Christmas period - can also work.

The second can actually be more powerful: loss aversion. The feeling you may miss out on something is an immensely powerful human drive. Far more powerful than the chance to receive something. It's known these days as FOMO - fear of missing out.

Companies use this all the time in promotions. For example, sign-ups to a free trial period at a paid-for website increased by 102% when the length of the free trial was reduced from 28 days to 14 days.[55]

So, when applying it to charity, an easy way to push this button is to do a matched giving campaign for a fixed period of time – let's say a week. This might be using money a corporate donor has committed to give you anyway, but you can show them how you're using their cash intelligently to win even more income, as well as boosting their reputation in the process.

Alternatively, Local Giving do a matched funding campaign each year. You could also give away a free invite to your next big fundraiser event, but only to the next three donors. Things like that.

Remove barriers

People like to give themselves excuses for not doing, or putting off doing, the right thing. This is especially true if it costs them money or effort. Like the effort of walking away from their computer and digging out their credit card from their purse. This might seem like a trivial task, but it's still a barrier and any barrier, no matter how minor, can be used as an excuse.

If you can guess what these barriers might be, or even ask people what they are, you can then drip-feed content and messages out with your channels in order to counteract these ideas gradually.

Common ones for UK digital donors are:

"My money will matter just as much next week, I'll give later."

"My donation probably won't go on the cause anyway."

"This problem is too big to make much of an impact on."

"It's not secure giving my card details to a small charity online."

"Some charities don't make a big difference."

Try and challenge these thoughts and misconceptions, ideally through stories or messaging that focuses on the real impact past donations have had through your work.

Bonus tip: Give eye contact

The last tip is specific to imagery, and the real power it has when it comes to donations if you do it well.

Digital fundraising allows us to test things like never before. We can make changes to a donation page quickly, and then show half of visitors one page, and the second half another version. We can then decide what change works best, and keep iterating until we've arrived at something much more effective. This is known as A/B testing - so if you are ever given the opportunity to do it, do it. You can get some fascinating insights about what gets your audience giving more.

Anyway, one unexpected outcome of this work, for some big charities with the resources to do this, is that they have found that using images of people looking at the donate button, or making eye contact with the potential donor during the 'ask', can actually increase the average gift amount per donation by as much as 48%.[56]

In another social experiment, whenever an image of 'watching eyes' was present in the vicinity of a collection jar for a local charity, the median donation amount increased by 500%.[57]

Oxfam actually ask their photographers to capture people looking to the camera, then in different directions, so they can use an image on their website that leads the viewer's eyeline to the next step that they want them to take. That might be a donation button, or a higher donation amount versus a smaller one.

Getting people to do it for you

As you can see, some activities in your strategy depend not on getting people to give to you, but on getting people to get other people to give to you.

This is an effective and efficient way to boost digital fundraising income that a lot of charities aren't maximising on.

- In an average peer-to-peer fundraising campaign, 15-18% of donations are referred directly from Facebook.[58]

- 39% of people whose friends post about a charitable donation online subsequently donate themselves.[59]

- 43% 'like' a charity's Facebook page because family or friends have already liked it.[60]

- Emails about fundraising are opened 14% of the time[61]. To improve this, giving your sender ID a human name, rather than just your charity name e.g. John from Example Charity, increased both open rate and click-through rate by 8.1% respectively. Similarly, addressing the recipient by their name and using engaging, informal language increases the open rate by a further 139%.[62]

So, let's take a look at what we can do to encourage people to encourage others.

There are two key ways:

1. They can spread the word about you and your campaigns on their digital channels.

2. They can sign up to fundraise for you and collect sponsorship on their digital (and offline) channels.

Let's break those down a little bit though.

Ask them to do it

If you don't ask, you don't get.

It's likely you have people either shouting about you, or fundraising for you already, but don't stop at that.

Regularly ask people to get involved in spreading important messages.

People are most likely to get involved if it's something that matters to them, or if it helps towards a campaign that feels urgent, or one that has a large number of people behind it. Research found that, when a potential JustGiving donor is able to see the value of previous donations, it influences their own donation: for every £10 increase in the average of past donations, the next donor will, on average, increase their own gift by £2.50.[63]

Don't just ask them to do it

If the only time you get in touch with your supporters is when you want them to post to social media for you, email their friends, publish stuff on their website or do a sponsorship activity you're going to get limited results. You'll be like that friend who only shows up when they want something.

Instead keep the relationship warm and make your supporters feel special. Ask for influential supporters' opinions on new campaigns, or to give them an early heads up when you're about to do something special, make them feel part of your team and they'll act like part of the team.

Make it easy

By providing a mix of ways people can help you - from tweeting a campaign message to signing up to a big sporting sponsorship event - you'll maximise the number of people who are willing to help, as well as providing natural ways to progress relationships.

A lot of charities have Get Involved pages, which list a few simple ways to donate or fundraise. But it seems like everyone knows how to hold a bake sale or complete a marathon. What could you offer that's different?

Plus, trying different ways to get people to do this will mean you learn what works, and can add it to your campaign calendar, and what doesn't

Learn from Plumpy'Nut

A great example of getting people to raise funds for you is the Plumpy'Nut challenge by Merlin - the international aid charity that has now merged with Save the Children.

They wanted to give people an excuse to raise sponsorship funds in a way that was easy, that didn't take loads of training, and that would be inherently social media friendly.

They offered Twitter users the chance to sign up to receive a box of four Plumpy'Nut sachets, a nutrition-packed peanut paste that's used in famine relief areas to fight malnutrition.

The challenge was to survive on nothing but Plumpy'Nut for the day, tweet about it, and ask for sponsorship money on Virgin Money Giving.

The campaign was novel, it got people talking, and almost anyone could do it. Some people even chose to do it for more than one day to raise more sponsorship.

It took social media by storm and raised £40,000. A fantastic total for a low-budget campaign from a small charity.

Be current

Everyone obsessed about the Bake Off? That means they've got baking on the mind and probably want to give it a go. They're already half-sold on doing something, perhaps even getting involved in a charity bake sale. How can you build on that?

Think about what's current nationally, and what's a hot topic in your area. Can you use that as a base of interest to build on? Engaging your supporters in something they enjoy will be much easier than trying to interest them in trying something new.

Be diverse

Different people like different things. For some people, life revolves around their triathlon time, for others it's family time.

Have different sponsorship things for different types of target audience. Build a portfolio of what works for you.

If you can find things that are easy for people to do sat at their computer, or out and about with their mobile phone, then even better!

Monitor

Keep an eye on your supporter base for anyone with big Twitter feeds, loads of Facebook friends, a popular YouTube channel, a big mummy blog, a massive Instagram following, a job at a media outlet, etc. Check people out on social media if you get notified that they've set up a fundraising page too.

MailChimp does some of this work for you if you pay a small fee, by scanning your mailing list for people with big followings on social media. Automation can be a quick timesaver, but manual checks are the only way to be sure, though.

When it comes to other platforms, learn to become a master of search. Use Google and Google Blog search to find blogs focused on your cause and start up a relationship. You can also use the Twitter and YouTube search features to the same effect, with tools like Twellow, that help you find like-minded individuals on Twitter too. These are all good starting points. Twitter allows you to search particular geographic areas too, which is great to help a local charity, or branch, find influential people in their catchment areas.

Go where they are

If you're trying to attract more people likely to fundraise, where are they online?

If it's a family event, maybe you should be interacting on Mumsnet more? Got a classic car thing going on every year, do you interact on Pistonheads? Need to fill places on running events, which fitness social media feeds are you following?

Educate

If you want people to raise money for you then make sure they know how to do it.

Do they know they can set up an online fundraising page for free on JustGiving? Since its inception, JustGiving has enabled over £2.1 billion worth of donations to over 13,000 charities and they're growing every year, so it's important to have a presence on their platform if you don't already.[64]

And that's not the only thing you can do. Do your supporters know what hashtag you use to fundraise? Or that they can record a marathon training video diary using their phone?

If you don't have the time or the resources to create content on these topics yourself, you can usually point to other content online. Though it's worth pointing out that useful content like this is always useful to have on your site from an SEO perspective.

> *"Here's how you make a video diary of your marathon training."*

> *"Here's how you promote your JustGiving page on your Facebook account."*

> *"Five tips to boost your sponsorship pages."*

> *"Motivational quotes to inspire you to get training for the 10k!"*

> *"What is Gift Aid, and can I donate it?"*

> *"What platforms can I use to raise money?" (i.e. other than JustGiving?)*

Recognise

Any time someone does something for you, make sure you thank them.

This falls into "tips that are so obvious, that your mum first told you this when you were three". However, the reality is most charities are shockingly bad at this. How bad? Well we ran a test to find out. We made moderately large donations to ten charities one after another.

And of those ten, only one of them made a proper thank you.

If you're that one charity, then you're going to create a feeling of goodwill in your donors. Don't just reserve it for donations though. Do it whenever someone gives you something positive. Take social media – someone sending a quick tweet of support might feel like nothing, but if you thank them for it, maybe they'll do something bigger next time.

Celebrate

When people do a good job on your behalf, show-off the results of it to other supporters to create social proof around that behaviour, and to make the supporter feel great about what they did.

Be careful not to overdo this, though, and spam every little Facebook post or Tweet out to all your social media channels. Better to do it just for the key actions, like when someone hits a fundraising goal or writes a blog post, or gets in the local paper etc.

Incentivise

You may need to incentivise people to get the most out of them.

Often the best way to do this is with cost-free activities. This could be by promising to feature people that keep a video diary or set up a JustGiving page on your social media accounts (telling them how many thousands of people will see their efforts often helps with this).

It may be you're putting on an event and you can give a few supporters free 'VIP' tickets for very little additional cost.

Or you might be able to find a high-net-worth or corporate sponsor to provide a prize, such as a month's free pass to a local cinema, VIP admission to an event, a free trip, etc. for your top sponsor(s).

You're almost there

By now you should be a social master. At least in theory.

You know how to get people to listen to you and like you. You've stopped talking about yourself all the time and you're interacting with people and crafting real relationships.

But now it's time to get a little bit more technical. It's time to build on these skills and learn how to increase those donations, in both amount and frequency. It's time to turn those initial few donations into a steady stream of income for your campaign or charity.

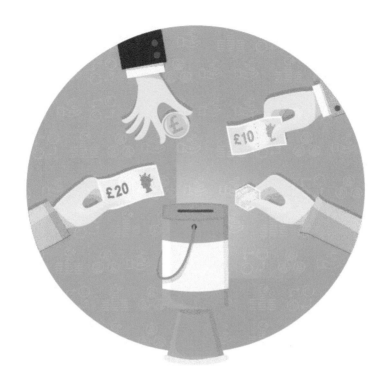

Chapter 6

Get more people giving

Overview

Let's imagine the world of digital donations is a singles' bar. You go in alone, knowing no one, not knowing what to expect and, if you're honest with yourself, terrified at the prospect of meeting new people. But you take a deep breath and you walk through that door. Inside, you see a bunch of people that you like the look of. Awesome. But you're not the only one, everyone is vying for the attention of everyone else.

You've got the moves though; you already know how to attract people's attention, you already know how to be interesting, you already know how to make people believe in you and your cause. You've got them hanging off your every word. It's time to go in for the big ask:

Will you donate with me?

And it's not just about the question itself, but how you ask it. There are still conversion techniques you can use to seal the deal, and turn your followers into donors once they are on your website.

By the end of this chapter, we'd like you to feel like a fundraising casanova, basically.

Conversion rate optimisation

Conversion rate optimisation isn't the nicest term to get your head around, but it's one of those things that's much simpler than it sounds.

If you're looking to turn more people into "donors" instead of just visitors, readers, followers, fans or subscribers then what you're thinking of doing is some 'conversion rate optimisation', or CRO.

CRO is the practice of increasing the conversion rate - the percentage of visits to a page that result in someone giving a donation.

This percentage tends to be very small, so don't be disheartened if it's less than half a percent. Even tiny increases quickly add up when applied to thousands of visitors over a period of months.

There are some things that you can change to optimise your conversion rate - the ask, the action and the conversion point itself. The ask and the action are often referred to together as the 'call to action' or CTA.

Boosting your conversion rate

Imagine you're reading a story on a charity's website, maybe even your website. It started out with a compelling hook, it took you on an emotional journey, and you ended up angry and wanting to do something. What next?

Leaving readers with the feeling that they need to click on a link and give you money is key to conversion.

The piece of text that bridges you from the content you're reading to the action you need to take is the 'ask'.

Crucially, this text needs to include an 'action' for the user to perform, such as a link to click.

For example, once a user clicks a link to donate, they're presented with a form for their bank details – the 'conversion point'.

If the form is easy to fill-in and looks trustworthy, then they'll likely go through the process of completing it.

Now, if you can improve your ask, action and conversion point, then your conversion rate will increase.

So, let's say you have 100 people a day reading a page on your website about the impact of your charity on a service user, and your conversion rate of this page is 0.25% with an average gift of £25. If we could increase this rate to just 1% (which is achievable on a page like this) that would increase your yearly income from this page from £2,281 to £9,125.

So, how do you do that?

Better asks

Improving the piece of text – or audio, or video, in the case of multimedia content – that bridges the user to the action you want them to take is an easy start to increasing conversion rates. Small changes and improvements can make a big difference.

Actually ask

Too many charity websites, web pages and social media feeds don't feature any calls to action at all, so just having a simple link at the bottom of a page encouraging people to donate is a good start.

Make it visible

A call to action at the end of the article makes sense. However, if you're writing good web copy it's likely you're using the 'inverted pyramid' style. This is where you put the important and engaging information at the beginning, in case readers don't read further down to get to the detail. Bearing this in mind, it makes sense to repeat the call to action during the second or third paragraph, to ensure that people see it even if they don't read on.

Be specific

Generic calls to donate are far less effective than an ask that flows with the text, and links the story or issue the person is reading about with the action you want them to take. You've spent hours putting together a piece of web content, so why skimp on the five minutes it would take to make a bespoke call to action?

Cancer Research UK combining 'social proof' and 'urgency' on their homepage.

Be persuasive

Follow the persuasion techniques we talked about earlier in chapter five, and ensure your ask doesn't just describe the action you want people to take, but actually works to persuade them to do it. Tools like 'social proof' and 'urgency' work well for this.

Motivate

Your text must not only persuade, but it must avoid being demotivating. Be careful not to turn people off. The classic mistake here is talking about how much money per day you need to keep operational. Not only does that make the would-be-donor's £20 look like a drop in the ocean, but it's not inspiring to know that you're money is purely for "keeping the organisation operating".

The same logic can be applied to how your social media accounts should be run. 43% of responses to a recent survey reported 'unliking' a charity's Facebook page due to the charity posting too much and, crucially, 36% reported doing so because the charity only posted appeals for donations.[65]

The water crisis.

663 million people still live without clean water in developing countries around the world. Many walk 2-4 hours a day to swamps and rivers to gather dirty water for their families.

About our work.

Since charity: water started in 2006, we've funded projects in countries around the world that have brought clean water to millions of people. Join us. Pledge your birthday.

72,342 people have already pledged.   PLEDGE NOW

Show your supporters something they can be a part of.

Focus on your users

You can avoid being demotivating by being user-centric. Put yourself in the reader's shoes. What would you want to hear to make you take an action? What is it about your cause, or your users' needs that compels people? Don't just talk about the organisation's needs. It gets boring pretty quickly.

Better actions

The choice of the action you want people to take is another key factor that determines how many people go through with the conversion.

Add links

Asking someone to pick up the phone or print something, fill it in and post it back hardly ever works.

A recent project we worked on, building a customisable lottery website for hospices, unearthed some fascinating stats. Lotteries tend to account for 5-15% of a given hospice's annual income, but many are relying on either offline sign-ups, or cumbersome and flawed online sign-up processes. We calculated that, if a typical hospice's lottery sign-up process was optimised fully, plays would increase to account for as much as 54% of their annual income – much better than asking a supporter to download, print, complete, and post something back to you!

If you are fundraising then link to a page where users can donate, if you are looking for volunteers then add a link to an online sign-up form. Simple.

Be action-focused

The eye is drawn to links - they're in a different colour and underlined to catch our attention. This has the effect of emphasising them to the reader. Make the most of that by using inspirational, action-focused words; not "click here".

Track it

Google Analytics tracks the links that are clicked on your website. So making sure you keep an eye on which links get the most clicks will give you insights into which 'calls to action' are working best, and which pieces of content.

Isolate

Don't overwhelm with options. Have a clear default option to avoid the paradox of too much choice causing decision paralysis, losing you valuable potential donations.

Don't always be direct

Rather than asking for a high value action there and then (like a regular direct debit donation, sometimes it's better to find a way to get a user's email address or phone number, and follow up with them later when you've deepened the relationship.

Better conversion points (forms)

Improving the form itself is the last thing you can do to increase your donation conversion rates, and perhaps the most significant. It's unlikely you'll be able to action these changes yourself, so you can see the below as a checklist for testing your website and making a list of improvements to pass to your web manager or digital agency.

Keep it snappy

Shorter forms are better at converting people into donors than longer ones.

The fundraising page for Obama's presidential election campaign in 2012 is a great example of this. In an attempt to optimise donations, they shortened their one-page, fourteen-field donations page into four, small steps – each one on a different page, and each with just a single form field to complete. The result was a 5% rise in conversion rate, which is an amazing result for such a small change.[66]

Optimised donation process resulted in a 5% rise in conversion rate, for Obama's presidential election campaign.

So the fewer fields you have the better. The tradeoff is that fewer fields means less donor data. A way to manage this is to make some fields 'conditional', for example only showing a dedication message field if the user specifies they're giving as a dedication/tribute. You might also want to think if there's any data you can capture after the transaction has gone through, perhaps using post-payment form fields or an email survey.

Stay on-site

Don't jump the user to another site if you can help it; keep the donation payment process integrated into your site. This has a cost attached to it, so it's only worth doing if your donation volume justifies it. However, if it does, then it should be very high up your website wishlist.

Make it accessible

Don't ask your would-be donor to register and log in first. Few users will want to create an account and this functionality is only a benefit to repeated one-off donors. If you do want to offer the ability to create an account, it's better to make this an optional checkbox after the process.

Be trustworthy

More than 1 in 3 people have some mistrust in UK charities[67]. So, it goes without saying that your donation forms need to be secure, and that means that they are protected by an SSL Certificate (which causes the person's web browser to display a tiny padlock, usually in the address bar). Few users are educated about this, however, so much so that simply putting an image of a padlock on the donation form page can increase conversions. In fact, when Oxfam tested this it resulted in an extra £2.09 per donation due to increase in conversion rate and average amount.[68]

Remove distractions

Have you ever been casually browsing on the internet, just wasting time, decided to have a look on Amazon, then ended up at the checkout with a basket full of things? That's no coincidence, the people at Amazon know their stuff and everything on that site serves one purpose: getting you to buy. As soon as you put an item in your basket, they've pretty much sealed the deal. Their checkout has no distractions, it's focused, simple and efficient.

So take a page from their book and do the same for your forms and donation processes. Hide navigation items, sidebars and footer links. Remove anything that can steal away people's attention. Make it so the only thing to do is to proceed to the next step in the process.

Forgive mistakes

Even the most tech-savvy amongst us will miss, or mistype, fields from time to time. So plan for mistakes. If a would-be donor keys in an incorrect card number make sure all other details are retained when the page reloads, and that the error message is friendly and makes it obvious exactly what needs to be corrected to proceed. You may even want to display a phone number, email address or live chat option in case the user needs further help or wants to report a technical fault with your site.

Make it semantic

Most web browsers and devices now offer to automatically complete personal and credit card details, or offer a faster way to look-up your address by entering your postcode. In order to do this, the form must be coded in a 'semantic' way. Test this on your own form, as it can be the difference between someone donating or not, when they can't be bothered to go and get their card from their wallet in another room.

Be mobile friendly

With around 50% of traffic to most charity websites coming from mobile devices, it's more important than ever that your forms work well on mobile. And yet, a 2014 study found that just 62% of 50 big charity websites they looked at had been optimised for mobile. So there's still some work to be done.[69]

You may even wish to tailor the mobile experience further by reducing the number of form fields to complete. Simplify your forms as much as possible to ensure that all users go through with the altogether more awkward process of filling a form in on their mobile phone.

It's also a ranking factor for SEO now, thanks to Google's update from April 2015, where mobile-friendly pages are being boosted in search results.

Better donation options

Your supporters have to trust you'll spend their money wisely, and a lot of this comes down to your past work establishing relationships. However, there's a few tricks you can use to increase the average donation amount.

These five tactics mainly apply to an on-site donation process, but they're also equally as relevant to crowdfunding campaigns.

Suggest donation amounts

Don't leave it to your donor to decide what to give—suggest amounts. Having three amounts at varying price points work best. Each option should help the donor understand what their money **could** achieve. We use the word "could" very deliberately to avoid giving a guarantee that we'll actually spend the money on that exact activity.

Make higher donations seem better value

When buying a TV you might have noticed that the cheaper option is often poor value, because it's has fewer features than the mid range option for marginally less money. This is a deliberate strategy to make the higher priced TVs feel better value, whilst still giving a cheap option for those without the means to afford a better one.

This same strategy can be employed with online donation amounts. When crafting your explanations of what each amount could do, make the higher amounts look like better value. Don't say £2 for a malaria pill could save a life, and a £100 could fund an hour of education, for example.

Plan your amounts

Your three price points should be spaced apart, with a low, medium and high option. The ideal is to push your donor slightly higher than what they would have picked themselves. Drawing a graph of your current donation amounts and adding a few pounds to the three 'spikes' that best match to low, medium and high amounts is a good way to do this.

Round off your numbers

Once you've come up with your ideas for amounts you should round them to psychologically attractive amounts. For example £30 is more likely to be picked than £27. Oxfam tested round numbers against ones that seemed more precise, such as £100 vs £120. They found that rounder numbers worked better, and were worth an extra £1.28 per donation to them.[70]

Offer incentives

A relatively new strategy, which is proving extremely effective, is incentivisation. Especially in crowdfunding, or competitions where multiple entries can be bought in exchange for donations. Would-be donors arrive thinking of giving you a small contribution to show support, but are shown a 'ladder' of suggested amounts – the higher the amount, the better the incentive.

For competitions, this is often bonus entries. For crowdfunding, it might be tickets to special events for higher contributions. The best rewards are ones that cost you little-to-nothing, for example a cup of tea with your CEO might be the difference between a £100 and £500 contribution, depending on how valuable it's perceived to be by your donors.

Finding the balance

Conversion rate optimisation is usually straightforward, especially when it comes to asks and actions. Even modest increases will have a big difference on your annual digital fundraising total. Getting the best conversion rate optimisation can be a balancing act though.

Sometimes, it makes sense to actively reduce your conversion rate if it means you can get a bigger payoff now or later. For example, say you reduce your conversion rate by half but those that do convert give an average of three times as much.

Conversely, it's easy to improve your conversion rate by asking for a petition signature instead of a monetary donation, but it's not going to help your fundraising goals.

A holistic digital fundraising strategy focuses just as much on making the most of existing traffic as it does driving more traffic to your website, page or message. The best results though, come from doing both together.

Sadly, there's no one combination of words or form design layout that gets people giving the most. Each cause and audience is unique, so try out the techniques here in different ways and see what works with your audiences.

The strategy section at the end of the book includes a section on conversion rate optimisation, with suggested actions and space to fill in your own numbers to work out potential gains.

Are we done yet?

It's the end of chapter six. And you probably deserve a pat on the back for sticking with us.

We'd like to say that it's the end and your certificate will be in the post, but we have a final chapter for you. It's not more information for you to absorb, or make notes on. It's actually a chapter that will bring everything we have discussed to life through examples.

Because what's the point in just talking about it? Let's make it happen.

Chapter 7
Bring it all together

Overview

So you've made it this far; you now know all the types of fundraising, you know what tools you need to use to make the most of them, you know how to reach and engage your audience, you know how to persuade them to keep listening, and you know how to make the most of them.

It's great to have that knowledge, but if it's not applicable in the real world then what would be the point in it (apart from trivia for the most obscure pub quizzes)? Fortunately, everything we've talked about in the past six chapters is more than just theory. It's been tried, tested and proven by charities fundraising across the globe. So let's look at some real-world examples that have put it into practice using a variety of fundraising mechanics.

Royal Hospital for Neuro-disability's Brain Awareness Week Campaign

Our brains are the most important things in our world. That ball of squishy tissue not only controls what we do, but defines who we are. That's why the Royal Hospital of Neuro-disability (RHN), a national charity based in London, treat and care for people who are affected by brain injuries and degenerative neurological conditions.

This campaign from RHN was a great example of how to use emotion and technology.

In 2013, RHN wanted to run a campaign to raise £20,000 in order to provide more assisted technology sessions for people suffering from the effects of a stroke or locked-in syndrome, as well as Parkinson's, Alzheimer's, and other disabilities.

With this campaign they wanted to use their existing donor and contact database, as well as reach some new, younger donors. So they took the step to go digital and contacted us. Together we looked at what assets RHN had.

They had a business sponsor who was willing to give £10,000, they had strong service user and staff stories, they had a volunteer with video skills. Finally, they had the perfect opportunity to use the popularity of another campaign to boost theirs: Brain Awareness Week, a global event to raise awareness and celebrate the progress of brain research. By looking at these assets, the foundations for a successful campaign were laid.

As technology is so important to RHN's patients, it made sense that it would be the focal point for the entire campaign. We made three videos to communicate the emotional element of the appeal, which focused on the stories of users – on the people who would benefit from any money raised from the appeal.

Each video highlighted that people living with locked-in syndrome and other extreme neurodisabilities are people just like everyone else and, with support, RHN can help these people communicate again.

By using video not only was the information easily digestible for the viewer, not only did it allow people to see the impact that donations would have, but it also created a connection between the viewer and the people they would be helping in a way no other media could. To view a video, people would have to view it on a phone, a tablet or a computer; technology just like what was being used at the hospital to support people with locked-in syndrome. It showed how the technology the donor uses is used by people at the hospital for a radically different, more profound use.

The videos were supported with strong written content and CTAs that demonstrated the real effects that donations could have. It was all hosted on the charity's website, which was new and had little-to-no passive traffic. The charity had a limited Twitter and Facebook presence, and a moderate donor and contact mailing list.

It was pretty much a blank slate. So we used Reddit to host a Q&A (called an AMA or Ask Me Anything). We also sent press releases to various blogs and news sites (with a focus on technology and disability) and had pick-up from a few, including T3 magazine.

The campaign used a single and a regular ask mechanic, but mainly drove people to single asks to capture as many people as possible. There was also text giving as a back-up ask. To add urgency and encourage people to donate, a matched-giving incentive was set up for the duration of Brain Awareness Week – any donations made in those seven days were doubled. Finally, a totaliser with a target of £20,000 was added.

We built a tool to show we used Thunderclap – a service that gets all signed-up people to tweet/Facebook at the same moment. As a result, Boris Johnson saw and re-tweeted the tweet.

RHN Charity @RHNcharity   11 Mar
Our new #BAW13 campaign film is live! See it on our new
charity website here: bit.ly/Y5bBug & tell us what #TechnologyMeans
to you
🔁 Retweeted by Boris Johnson
Expand

The tweet that was retweeted by Boris Johnson.

In that one week the campaign raised over £20,000. But not only that, it also created relationships with new donors, it increased subscribers to all of RHN's social media channels and won the 'Best Use of Technology' award at the 2013 Charity Times Awards.

John Underwood's fundraiser for Anthony Nolan

It's often said that content is king, and when it's done well, we would agree.

John Underwood went to his GP with what he thought was a vomiting bug, and was instead rushed to hospital and diagnosed with a very rare late-stage lymphoma.

So he set-up a fundraising page on JustGiving on behalf of Anthony Nolan, a charity that works to save the lives of people with blood cancer.

How was he trying to fundraise?

"I'm [trying not to die] for Anthony Nolan because [to be honest, I'm doing it for me too.]"

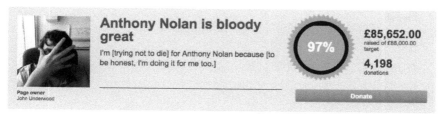

Anthony Nolan is bloody great

I'm [trying not to die] for Anthony Nolan because [to be honest, I'm doing it for me too.]

97%

£85,652.00
raised of £88,000.00 target

4,198
donations

Page owner
John Underwood

Donate

John Underwood captured supporters with great content.

His 'pitch', if you like, was everything a good charity pitch should be. It was honest, human, it gave you a reason to give, and it gave you an alternative if you couldn't. It was incredibly well-written, powerfully delivered, and, most importantly, real. John brought his situation, a situation many of us are blind to, until it happens to us, to life. He was open, candid and, in turn, he made people think.

Not only was his writing brilliant, but his ongoing fundraising effort is also something many charities could learn from.

He wasn't in it just for him, he wanted to help other people too. He wasn't afraid to ask, but when he did he did it creatively and timely. He shared milestones, so his supporters could see their efforts grow. And he still hasn't stopped thanking people.

We'd suggest you read it for yourself (give it a Google), while also checking out the latest fundraising total. At the time of writing this very sentence (mid-October 2015 if you were wondering), John has managed to raise over £85,000. An impressive £22,000 of that figure was raised in the first 48 hours. Not only that, over 1,400 people applied to join the stem cell register during the first week - 46% up on normal.[71]

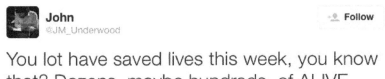

A great example of how to thank supporters on social media.

So what can you learn from this?

No, charities can't expect to have a service user writing powerful content and raising funds for them, all while hooked-up to chemotherapy treatment as he types. To be honest, who would want someone to be in that position at all? But this example isn't about finding someone to recreate this for you, it's an example that can teach you the power of content.

John's story shows what we've already discussed throughout this book – people are much more invested in a personal story over stats, people value storytelling and good writing, and people also value the honesty that comes with that.

We hope John manages to beat his lymphoma – that's one result we're still waiting on.

Bentley's Power on Ice

This was another campaign we worked on. It was a smaller, experimental campaign, ahead of something bigger so we could learn about conversion rates, average gifts, and test the effectiveness of different messaging.

The homepage for the Care2Save and Bentley Power on Ice campaign.

Bentley gave a three-day winter driving experience to a hospice charity called Care2Save, associated with a hospice.

The audience was the hospice's existing donor and contact database and Bentley's wider social media audience.

People could have a chance to win this experience by making a donation of just £1 with their credit or debit card online.

However, we wanted to see the effect of giving people more chances to win the more they donated. So £10 didn't give you 10 entries, but 12, and so on. As donations got higher, we also offered other incentives, such as a Bentley factory tour if someone donated £1,000. An entrant took advantage of this option too.

The competition was run as a "free prize draw, with paid entry option", so there was a 'enter for free' link in the footer.

The competition was open for seven weeks over the quiet Christmas period—not the ideal time—but this was a test and we needed a fast turnaround.

The conversion rate was a little under 5%, and the average gift was £15.09—both extremely high. The total raised was just into five figures.

Martha Payne's NeverSeconds

Do you recognise this young lady? No? You might recognise her blog.

Martha Payne's blog, 'Never Seconds'.

Her name is Martha Payne and in 2012, aged 9 years-old, she was set a writing project at her school in Argyll, Scotland. While most kids would write about their favourite cartoons or what they want to be when they grow up, there was something that bugged Martha: the dinners that her school offered. So she took the project as an opportunity to say something about them. With the help of her dad, she set up a blog called NeverSeconds and started writing about and taking pictures of her school meals.

Martha's surprisingly mature writing style and the novelty of the situation quickly caught the attention of the local press who subsequently ran headlines about the story. For seven weeks NeverSeconds was a fairly local story until Argyll and Bute council, fearing the negative press, banned her from updating it. People were outraged. They began spreading the news on Twitter where it reached celebrity chef Nick Nairn who protested the ban. It became a trending topic across the UK and came to the attention of Jamie Oliver who tweeted his support. That's when the national newspapers picked it up. It became a story known all across the world.

Where did that leave Martha and the council? The council quickly rescinded their ban, noting it was a mistake. Martha happily started blogging again and started raising money for Mary's Meals – a Scottish-based hunger relief charity. With the newfound attention, she raised £143,000[72]

So was this all down to luck? Was it just a fluke? Let's have a look.

Martha set up her blog because she felt there was some injustice, and she wanted somewhere to express how she felt about that. She posted interesting, funny, and shocking content about how horrible her some of her school dinners were. She posted about it on social media. And worked up relationships with influencers (the local media) who then promoted it. At this point she became well-known locally.

Argyll and Bute council then added further injustice. At this point though, she had an audience and influencers. She, along with her fans (including Nick Nairns and Jamie Oliver) took to Twitter to express outrage. Then, when her popularity was at its peak, she decided to set up a page to raise money for a school canteen in Africa. She used the audience she'd developed to promote the campaign to them. That's how a small blog from Argyll managed to raise nearly £150,000.

So, it seems we could all learn a thing or two from a 9 year-old about fundraising!

Alzheimer's Research UK doing it well, all the time

ARUK have a site that maximise donations every day.

While campaigns are the more exciting way to raise funds, there's a lot to be said for what you do day-to-day.

We wanted to include an example of a charity who maximised their donations process – Alzheimer's Research UK (ARUK).

We worked on ARUK's new website in 2015, helping them to create a site that would help them in their quest to find a cure for dementia.

This site is a clear example of maximising all of the areas we have discussed throughout this book.

It increased conversion rates, by considering user journeys in detail, taking on board a lot of what we spoke about in chapter three. The site features tailored call-to-actions throughout, which meant the donation process was promoted at key moments, with messaging bespoke to each step in the user's journey.

At the same time, research found that storytelling and sharing knowledge were two content elements that were crucial to gaining new supporters and donations. So we made sure ARUK had a platform from which to share their stories, using custom design layouts to immerse their users in the cause.

Given the growing popularity of mobile fundraising (30% of those who made donations on their mobile phones wouldn't have made them otherwise), we also made sure that text giving was featured prominently throughout the site, even more so when accessed by a mobile phone.

As covered in chapter six, Google Analytics was implemented so that ARUK can track their income and monitor what is working for them, and what isn't. This kind of information informs their fundraising strategy, not just digitally, but across the organisation, helping them to make better decisions in the future.

A key element that ARUK does very well is content. The fundraising area, which features plenty of ideas, a calendar, and a map, gives supporters no excuse not to get involved. And ARUK is able to fully establish itself as a thought leader in this area of research, with many research projects looking into causes, diagnosis, risks, symptoms and treatments; all available for the general public to see.

Yes, it may not be as exciting as a campaign involving bucket loads of ice and celebrities, but if you don't concentrate on the day-to-day that's a little bit like waiting all year for Christmas. There's plenty that happens in-between, and even if your conversion rate only goes up by a fraction of a percentage, that's still a fair bit of money when you consider there's another 364 days in a year.

#NoMakeUpSelfie and The Ice Bucket Challenge

No doubt many of you had your interest in digital fundraising re-ignited by seeing the stunning, unexpected success of the Ice Bucket Challenge. Or perhaps for some of you it was the #NoMakeUpSelfie phenomenon a few months earlier.

The Ice Bucket challenge raised over $100 million for the ALS Association in the US, and its UK counterpart, the MND Association, raised £7 million off the back of it.[73]

Everyone involved with a charity has, at some point, wondered: "How can we make our digital fundraising campaign go viral like the Ice Bucket Challenge?" The truth is, that would almost be impossible to engineer.

Your efforts would be much better spent building the best

relationships with your supporters that you can. Then, if one of them ends up coming up with the next big idea, or just wants to raise money for a different charity on the next social media fundraising bandwagon, they'll think of you first.

However, you can be more strategic.

When the #NoMakeUpSelfie challenge happened it must have caused lots of discussion and activity at Macmillan, especially as so many had previously used #NoMakeUpSelfie to raise funds and awareness of cancer. They weren't the biggest winners though; Cancer Research UK raised £8 million, whereas Macmillan failed to capitalise fully on this opportunity.

It's likely Macmillan wrote a strategy about how to make the most of it next time. This was probably pre-approved by management or the trustees so they could react at the speed that this social media phenomenon emerged at. Otherwise, by the time the next board meeting happened the whole thing would be over.

One of the most popular Ice Bucket Challenge videos was from Anthony Carbajal who was diagnosed with the disease along with his mum.

When the Ice Bucket Challenge started getting big, they almost immediately published a page on their website about the "Macmillan Ice Bucket Challenge" and used Google AdWords and social media posts to drive people to it.

As a result they raised £4.5 million[74.]

And over to you...

Now we're at the end of this book, you should probably know that you will fail at digital fundraising repeatedly. But that's okay. Failure is a key part of learning to succeed in a new and evolving art form.

Don't beat yourself up about it. Digital fundraising isn't easy, and even large, well-resourced charities can struggle to make every campaign work, let alone engineer an Ice Bucket Challenge.

If you can develop a healthy attitude to failure, and an appetite for experimentation, you'll start to not just improve your digital fundraising practice, but actively enjoy it.

It's not just digital fundraising you're learning about, though. Every campaign provides you with more stats and insights about what gets your would-be digital (and non-digital) donors giving.

Don't think you can't excel at this because you're not the most technical person in the world. Knowing how to use a new social networking website is just a case of spending five minutes on YouTube these days. The key skills you need are the same as they always have been: your communication skills to build relationships, your intuition for what motivates donors to give, your will to create a donor journey that's as easy and satisfying as possible, and your ability to get your supporters fundraising for you.

Today is a great time to start doing more digital fundraising, building your audience and learning what gets them giving. That means all fundraisers will need to be digital fundraisers in the not too distant future. The DEC already saw more than half their donations come from only digital sources during the Syria 2013 Appeal.

'Just as the web overtook newspapers, digital fundraising will overtake traditional methods. As our population ages, and old donors die off, the public will become increasingly hostile towards old-school techniques. Intrusive offline fundraising doesn't have a place in a world of digital communication that people are used to being in control of and participating directly within.

You've chosen to embrace this change and dive into digital fundraising and we can't wait to experience the digital campaigns you come up with.

Final Note

If you come up with a great fundraising campaign or insight - as a result of this book, or not - we'd love to hear about it to help spread the word and maybe even include it in our next edition.

Let us know by emailing us at: fundraisingbook@reasondigital. com. Or by tweeting @ReasonDigital. We'd love to hear from you.

Digital Fundraising Planning

A guide to developing and implementing a digital/online fundraising plan

Use this guide as a basis to help you create an online fundraising strategy for your general income generation activity and for specific, targeted campaigns.

You can download this strategy online at
www.reasondigital.com/books/fundraising

Situational analysis

Write a summary about what you already know about your online fundraising situation. Think about: why you are looking to boost online income? How will you spend that income? Why do you need the money? What's in your favour? What obstacles do you face?

_____

_____

_____

_____

_____

_____

_____

_____

_____

Objectives

My digital fundraising target is:

£

Set this as 10% of your offline income if you're unsure.

By: dd/mm/yyyy

A year is good, or give yourself two if you haven't got much groundwork in place.

Strategies

To boost your online fundraising income you can focus on one or all three of these income streams. Set an objective for each strategy you will pursue, bearing in mind the digital fundraising target you've set.

If you're unsure how to work these figures out, consult the appropriate sections below for help.

Strategy #1 - Boost ongoing, general donations

I expect to raise £ [   ] from general digital giving through my website / fundraising tool / text codes during that period, (i.e. not via campaigns).

Strategy #2 - Boost ongoing, general sponsorship

I expect to receive £ [   ] from peer-to-peer sponsoring from digital fundraising platforms during that period (i.e. not via campaigns).

Strategy#3 - Run campaigns to boost income activity

This means I have £ [   ] I need to raise through campaign(s). *Overall target=(General giving + General sponsorship)*

I have the resources to run [   ] campaigns this period.

So on average I need to raise £ [   ] through each.

Audiences and target audiences

List the specific groups and types of people you have or wish to develop access to online. Give some insight into these groups, state where they might be online, and estimate how warm their relationship is with you.

If you want to plan at an advanced level, then estimate the number of people you may be able to reach, as well as the expected 'conversion rate' (the percentage of visitors to your site who donate to your cause). Finally, calculate what you expect the average gift amount to be, using past donations as a reference if possible.

	General			Advanced bit		
Audience group	Insight	Channels or hangouts	Relationship Level	Est' No. You Could Reach?	Conversion %	Av Gift / Sponsorship
Families of service users	Believe in our services. High conversion and average gift.	Our website, Facebook, Twitter and newsletter.	Hot	300	10	55
Local gym users	Unlikely to give but may fundraise in a race for a local charity.	Facebook. Google "keep fit" terms. Gym website. Running forums.	Cold	100	1	500

Channels & influencers

You reach an audience digitally through a 'channel'. List the channels you have access to, and think about what audiences might be reachable through that channel.

Also consider 'influencers'; people who have a large following or mailing list of the audiences you would like to reach.

General				Advanced bit		
Audience group	Type (mailing list, social, website, etc)	Your Channel Y/ N	Audiences	Est' No. You Could Reach?	Con- version %	Av Gift / Spon- sorship
Our website	Website	Y	Families of service users, service users, supporters.	12000	0.25	25
Newsletter	Mailing list	Y	Supporters, service users, families of service users	350	0.5	30
Sally's (volunteer) Twitter	Social	N	Sally's friends, local and national arts and crafts	11000	Low?	Low?

Assets

An asset is a valuable item, experience, person or story that could be useful in incentivising people to give, or to give more.

Asset	Description	Provided by (If applicable)	Appeals to (Audience)	Expires (Date)
Bread making day	Local bakery will teach two people how to make bread.	Tippingtons Family Bakery.	Families of service users, Bake Off fans, craft and cooking.	
Donald Smith	UK record holder for oldest person to run a marathon.	n/a	Fundraisers, sporty, gym goers, journalists	n/a

Improving ongoing donation activity

First work out your baseline by looking at how many monthly visits you have to your website, your conversion rate and the average gift. Then, we'll look at tactics to improve each of these.

Our *Monthly Visits* are

Our *Conversion rate* is   %

Our *Average Gift* is   £

Our Total Monthly ongoing donation is

Notes:

- *Get Monthly Visits to website for Google Analytics*

- *Work out Conversion Rate by:*

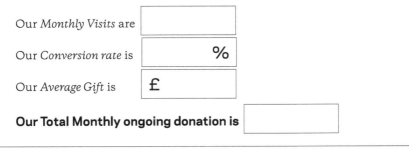

$$\frac{\text{Number of donations NOT FROM CAMPAIGNS}}{\text{Total number of visits to donation page}} \times 100$$

- *Work out Average Gift by:*

$$\frac{\text{Total amount given}}{\text{Number of donations}}$$

- *Work out Total Monthly ongoing donations by:*

Monthly visits x Conversion rate% x £ Average gift

- *Get total number of donations and total donation amount from fundraising platform/payment gateway.*

Tactics & actions

Think about how you can improve each metric and use the space below to set a time limit and assign responsibility for the task.

We will increase visitor numbers to our site by:

Task	Date	Person
Encouraging people to visit the site from newsletters and social media.		
Regularly adding interesting and/or useful posts to the website.		
Placing calls-to-action on printed materials, which include the website address.		
Placing links to the website in consistent email signatures for all staff.		

We will increase conversion rate by:

Task	Date	Person
Ensuring people can give online without a printable form or a phonecall.		
Adding calls to action through out the website pointing to the 'donate now' page.		
Improving the messaging in our "donate now" page.		
Trying persuasion techniques such as clear impact, social proof, donor benefits.		

We will increase our average gift by:

Task	Date	Person
Suggesting what different donation amounts could buy.		
Incentivising higher value donors with things that cost us little/nothing.		
Writing content that appeals to audiences that tend to give more and promoting it to them via relevant channels.		
Register for Gift Aid and input the number on our fundraising platform settings.		

Strategy #2

Improving ongoing donation activity

First work out your baseline by looking at how much you are likely to receive in ongoing sponsorship donations.

Number of people who choose to raise money for us	
Average donation per person	£
Our Total Monthly sponsorship income	£

Tactics & Actions

Think about how you can improve each metric and use the space below to set a time limit and assign responsibility for the task.

We will increase the number of people that choose our charity by:

Task	Date	Person
Registering our charity on the two main platforms (JustGiving and Virgin Money Giving), so people can find us when setting up a fundraising page		
Registering our charity on other fundraising platforms so people can find us there (Local Giving, BT MyDonate).		
Set up a "do a fundraising event" page(s):		
Publish useful or interesting content about fundraisers and/or for fundraisers on your website and share them on your other channels to attract relevant audiences.		

We will increase the number of people that choose our charity by:

Task	Date	Person
Emailing everyone that chooses us as a charity to encourage them.		
Putting pages on our site reminding fundraisers to share their fundraising page with their social media and email contacts.		
Signposting fundraisers to content about how they can create content for us such as video training diaries on YouTube?		
Offering to share the above content on our own channels to incentivise them to do this and boost the traffic to their fundraising pages.		

Resources

We estimate we need to allow for [   ] days of staff or volunteer

time to complete these actions and

£ [   ] of a budget, which we will spend on:

[   ]

My Campaign

(Create/print as many sheets as you have campaigns)

Campaign Target

Work out roughly how many donations you need to reach your campaign target, and how many people you need to see your campaign to generate that number of donations.

We want to raise £

We think the rough conversion rate of those exposed to the campaign would be: %

And that they will, on average, give (or raise in sponsorship) £ each (include a boost for Gift Aid if relevant).

This means we need to get $\dfrac{\text{Target}}{\text{Average gift}}$ = donations

This means we need to generate $\dfrac{\text{Target number of donations}}{\text{Conversion rate}}$

= views to out campaign

Audiences and channels

We will use our access to the following audiences to generate the interest we
need above:

Audience Group	How will they find out?	Why they will engage?	How will they support?
Families of service users	Our website. Our Facebook. Our Twitter. Our newsletter.	People like their parents and grandparents are facing this issue.	Give money. Share on Facebook. Tweet.
Local journalists	Twitter, personal email.	They want local, topical stories.	Publish campaign story on local paper website/social feeds.

Mechanic, Tools and Assets

What is the campaign *mechanic* and what *tool(s)* are needed to support this?

A campaign mechanic is a way someone interacts with your campaign to give you money. The main campaign mechanic types are listed below. Circle the one(s) you will use for this campaign.

Examples of campaign mechanics are:

Single / Regular / Text / Matched giving / Crowdfunding / Competitions & Lotteries / Cost-free / eCommerce & auctions / Traditional Sponsorship / Novel Sponsorship / Grassroots fundraising phenomena.

What tools will you need to support your mechanics, and promote, measure or manage your campaign?

Tool	Mechanic Type	Already using? Y/N	Cost?
JustGiving	Fundraising platform	Y	5% transaction fee
ThunderClap	Social media tool	N	None
Google Analytics	Visitor measurement	Y	None

The assets we will use are:

Which Asset?	How will you use them?	Why will they agree?	What effect will it have on the campaign?	Risks
Bread-baking day	Give attendance away as a prize.	Bakery is an existing supporter.	Increased number and value of donations. Increased engagement from social media. New donors.	We raise less than auctioning the ticket at the charity ball.

Key message(s) and call to action

What is the key campaign message?

What are you asking people to do?

What will be the wording of the call-to-action?

Campaign Content

What kind of content would support your campaign and on which channels?:

Content	Primary Channel	Promotion channel(s)	Formats	Person in charge of	Time / budget needed	Call to action
Interviews with service users at local food bank who have high energy bills.	Our website.	Twitter, Facebook, newsletter, local paper website.	Video, shocking quotes on Twitter	Sally Smith	10 hours volunteer time.	"Give now" link in video (through YouTube NFP programme.)

Resources

We estimate we need to allow for [ ] days' staff or volunteer time

to run this campaign and generate the content, and

£ [ ] of a budget which we will spend on:

[ ]

Campaign and activity calendar

Populate the calendar below with a rough idea of when you will run each campaign you're planning. Also, mark major actions, events or pieces of content on the calendar.

Jan	Feb	Mar	Apr

May	Jun	Jul	Aug

Sep	Oct	Nov	Dec

Bibliography

1.   Charity Aid Foundation (2014). UK Giving 2012/13 - an update. Available from:

    https://www.cafonline.org/about-us/publications/2014-publications/uk-giving-2013 [Accessed 8 Oct 2015].

2.   UK Online Giving Trends [online], 2015. - Institute of Fundraising. Available from:

    http://www.institute-of-fundraising.org.uk/guidance/research/uk-online-giving-trends/ [Accessed 8 Oct 2015].

3.   Blackbaud (2013) State of the Not-for-profit Industry Survey. [online]. Available from:

    https://hello.blackbaud.com/BBESoniReport.html [Accessed 8 Oct 2015].

4.   By Organizational Focus [online], 2015. LUMINATE ONLINE: Online Fundraising Software for Nonprofits. Available from:

    https://www.blackbaud.com/online-marketing/luminate-online-fundraising-software [Accessed 8 Oct 2015].

5.   Record digital gifts to Syria Appeal [online], 2013. Disasters Emergency Committee. Available from:

    http://www.dec.org.uk/press-release/record-digital-gifts-to-syria-appeal [Accessed 8 Oct 2015].

6.   Keep Aaron Cutting: Aaron's Story [online], 2015. Keep Aaron Cutting: Aaron's Story. Available from:

    http://keepaaroncutting.blogspot.co.uk/2011/08/aaron-biber-89-who-has-run-barber-shop.html [Accessed 8 Oct 2015].

7.   Roy C. Jones, CFRE [online], 2015. Roy C Jones CFRE. Available from:

http://royjonesreports.com/?p=2174 [Accessed 8 Oct 2015].

8. Mobile Powers Red Nose Day Fundraising – Mobile Marketing [online], 2015. Mobile Marketing Mobile Powers Red Nose Day Fundraising Comments. Available from: http://mobilemarketingmagazine.com/mobile-powers-red-nose-day-fundaraising/#o0c rbeqtuq6vxcqk.99 [Accessed 8 Oct 2015].

9. Red noses and text messages – UK Fundraising [online], 2015. UK Fundraising. Available from: http://www.fundraising.co.uk/2015/03/18/red-noses-and-text-messages/ [Accessed 8 Oct 2015].

10. Association of Fundraising Professionals (2014) Fundraising Effectiveness Survey Report. Available from: http://www.afpnet.org/files/ContentDocuments/FEP2014FinalReport.pdf [Accessed 8 Oct 2015].

11. Ten UK charity fundraising websites compared | Reason Digital [online], 2015. Reason Digital. Available from: http://reasondigital.com/advice-and-training/ten-uk-charity-fundraising-websites-compared/ [Accessed 22 Oct 2015].

12. Six UK payment gateways compared | Reason Digital [online], 2015. Reason Digital. Available from: http://reasondigital.com/advice-and-training/six-uk-payment-gateways-compared/ [Accessed 8 Oct 2015].

13. Registering and claiming [online], 2015. – Institute of Fundraising. Available from: http://www.institute-of-fundraising.org.uk/guidance/fundraising-essentials-legislation/tax-effective-giving/gift-aid/registering-and-claiming/ [Accessed 8 Oct 2015].

14. Social Networking: The UK as a Leader in Europe [online], 2015. – ONS.

Available from:

http://www.ons.gov.uk/ons/rel/rdit2/internet-access---households-and-individuals/
social-networking--the-uk-as-a-leader-in-europe/sty-social-networking-2012.html
[Accessed 8 Oct 2015].

15.   Adults' Media Use and Attitudes Report 2014 [online], 2015. Adults' Media Use
and Attitudes Report 2014. Available from:

http://stakeholders.ofcom.org.uk/market-data-research/other/research-publications/
adults/adults-media-lit-14/ [Accessed 8 Oct 2015].

16.   Adults' Media Use and Attitudes Report 2014 [online], 2015. Adults' Media Use
and Attitudes Report 2014. Available from:

http://stakeholders.ofcom.org.uk/market-data-research/other/research-publications/
adults/adults-media-lit-14/ [Accessed 8 Oct 2015].

17.   BBC News, 2015. [online]. BBC News. Available from:

http://www.bbc.co.uk/news/business-33712729 [Accessed 8 Oct 2015].

18.   The 2014 M R Benchmarks Study is Available for Download! [online], 2015.
M R 2014 Benchmarks. Available from:

http://mrbenchmarks.com/2014.html [Accessed 8 Oct 2015].

19.   Facebook fundraising part two: share more, raise more [online], 2013.
JustGiving blog. Available from:

http://blog.justgiving.com/facebook-fundraising-part-two/ [Accessed 8 Oct 2015].

20.   Ipsos MORI (2012). Public trust and confidence in charities (June 2012).
Available from:

https://www.gov.uk/government/uploads/system/uploads/attachment_data/
file/284715/ptc_ipsos_mori_2012.pdf [Accessed: 8 Oct 2015].

21.   Brother, can you spare a dime? Peer pressure in charitable solicitation [online],
2015. Brother, can you spare a dime? Peer pressure in charitable solicitation.

Available from:

http://www.sciencedirect.com/science/article/pii/s0047272710001866
[Accessed 8 Oct 2015].

22.   Optimising Your SEO Campaign Using Multi-Channel Funnels & Assisted Conversions | Branded3 [online], 2013. Branded3. Available from:

https://www.branded3.com/blog/using-content-strategy-to-increase-conversions-from-multi-channel-customers/ [Accessed 8 Oct 2015].

23.   The Nonprofit Partnership (2011). Nonprofit Communications Trends Report. Available from:

http://www.thenonprofitpartnership.org/files/2011-np-communication-trends.pdf
[Accessed: 8 Oct 2015].

24.   Six case studies and infographics on the optimal time to send emails [online], 2015. Econsultancy. Available from:

https://econsultancy.com/blog/62688-six-case-studies-and-infographics-on-the-optimal-time-to-send-emails/ [Accessed 8 Oct 2015].

25.   JustGiving donations surged by a quarter in 2014 [online], 2015. The Telegraph. Available from:

http://www.telegraph.co.uk/finance/newsbysector/mediatechnologyandtelecoms/digital-media/11320351/justgiving-donations-surged-by-a-quarter-in-2014.html
[Accessed 8 Oct 2015].

26.   Charity fundraising news – JustGiving Twitter donations grow by 70 per cent in a year [online], 2015. Civil Society. Available from:

http://www.civilsociety.co.uk/fundraising/news/content/16762/justgiving_twitter_donations_grow_by_70_per_cent_in_a_year [Accessed 8 Oct 2015].

27.   UK Online Giving Trends [online] 2015. Blackbaud. Available from:
https://www.blackbaud.co.uk/ukonlinegivingtrends [Accessed: 8 Oct 2015].

28.   ComRes (2014). CAF – Ice Bucket Challenge. Available from:
http://comres.co.uk/wp-content/themes/comres/poll/CAF_Ice_Bucket_Challenge_
Tables.pdf [Accessed: 8 Oct 2015].

29.   The Dynamics of Crowdfunding: An Exploratory Study [online], 2015. by Ethan
R. Mollick. Available from:
http://poseidon01.ssrn.com/delivery.php?id= 6120850860711060861140191090 1
00250780060400200610710330760930850970730950660690811091010030430
40006010034084028006112077067093061087094034004088102065087005125
02006402404905512406402707408402800802612203010209211806411008500
110106509708001909506601 6017 &ext=pdf [Accessed 8 Oct 2015].

30.   WE Communications [online], 2015. WE Communications. Available from:
http://waggeneredstrom.com/what-we-do/social-innovation/report-digital-persuasion/
[Accessed 8 Oct 2015].

31.   YouTube on Mobile: Viewers Sticking Around for 40 Minutes [online], 2015.
ReelSEO. Available from:
http://www.reelseo.com/youtube-mobile-increase-watch-time/ [Accessed 8 Oct 2015].

32.   4 Tactics for an Effective Video Content Marketing Strategy [online], 2013.
Content Marketing Institute. Available from:
http://contentmarketinginstitute.com/2013/03/video-content-marketing-effective-
strategy/ [Accessed 8 Oct 2015].

33.   16 Facts About Video Marketing That Will Keep You Up At Night [online], 2015.
Business 2 Community. Available from:
http://www.business2community.com/content-marketing/16-facts-video-marketing-
will-keep-night-0844491 [Accessed 8 Oct 2015].

34.   EyeView Digital. Increase Online Conversion Through Video. Available from:
http://www.eyeviewdigital.com/documents/eyeview_brochure.pdf. [Accessed: 8 Oct

2015]

35.   86% Of Charities And Nonprofits Use Twitter, 71% Say Social Useful For
Donations [STUDY] [online], 2015. SocialTimes. Available from:
   http://www.adweek.com/socialtimes/charity-nonprofit-social-media-study/499579
   [Accessed 8 Oct 2015].

36.   Charities shun internet advertising to focus on direct mail [online], 2015.
nfpSynergy News. Available from:
   http://nfpsynergy.net/press-release/charities-shun-internet-advertising-focus-direct-
   mail [Accessed 8 Oct 2015].

37.   Mobile vs Desktop: A Cross Device User Study – ShareThis.com [online], 2015.
ShareThiscom. Available from:
   http://www.sharethis.com/learn/knowledge-center/research-2/mobile-vs-desktop-a-
   cross-device-user-study/#sthash.ai912wcc.es3cqpy8.dpbs [Accessed 8 Oct 2015].

38.   65% of Time Spent on Social Networks Happens on Mobile [online], 2015.
Mashable. Available from:
   http://mashable.com/2013/10/24/content-consumption-desktop-
   mobile/#5cqlb26ej8kd [Accessed 8 Oct 2015].

39.   Infographic: Photos, Maps and Games Are Mobile-First Content [online], 2015.
Statista Infographics. Available from:
   http://www.statista.com/chart/1567/photos-maps-and-games-are-mobile-first-
   content/   [Accessed 8 Oct 2015].

40.   Tell us about yourself... | Twitter for Business [online], 2015. Tell us about
yourself... | Twitter for Business. Available from: https://business.twitter.com/resources/
tweetsmarter [Accessed 8 Oct 2015].

41.   Charities missing potential of social images and video [online], 2015. Charities
missing potential of social images and video. Available from:

http://www.prweek.com/article/1188841/charities-missing-potential-social-images-video [Accessed 8 Oct 2015].

42.   Ipsos MORI (2012). Public trust and confidence in charities (June 2012). Available from:

https://www.gov.uk/government/uploads/system/uploads/attachment_data/file/284715/ptc_ipsos_mori_2012.pdf [Accessed: 8 Oct 2015]

43.   Waggener Edstrom Worldwide Inc and Georgetown University (2012). Digital Persuasion:How social media motivates action and drives support. Available from: http://waggeneredstrom.com/downloads/DSCA-Summary.pdf. [Accessed 8 Oct 2015]

44.   Powell K.L., Roberts G. and Nettle D. (2012) Eye Images Increase Charitable Donations: Evidence From an Opportunistic Field Experiment in a Supermarket. Ethology, Vol 118 Issue 11. Available from:

https://www.staff.ncl.ac.uk/daniel.nettle/PowellRobertsNettle.pdf

45.   BrightSource (2012) What's stopping charities getting closer to their supporters?. Available from:

http://blog.brightsource.co.uk/sites/default/files/pdfs/2012/Whitepaper_SupporterCare.pdf. [Accessed: 8 Oct 2015]

46.   Campaign Monitor [online], 2015. 2015 Report: The New Rules of Email Marketing. Available from:

https://www.campaignmonitor.com/resources/guides/email-marketing-new-rules/ [Accessed 8 Oct 2015].

47.   Reason Digital (2015). An Insight Into the Charitable Giving of Young Adults & Students. Available from: http://reasondigital.com/wp-content/uploads/2015/09/result-document.pdf. [Accessed: 8 Oct 2015]

48.   The effect of information overload on consumer choice quality in an on-line environment [online], 2015. - Lee. Available from:

http://onlinelibrary.wiley.com/doi/10.1002/mar.20000/abstract [Accessed 8 Oct 2015].

49.   Online Information Review [online], 2015. The effect of information overload and disorganisation on intention to purchase online: The effect of information overload and disorganisation on intention to purchase online: : Vol 38, No 4. Available from:

http://www.emeraldinsight.com/doi/abs/10.1108/oir-01-2014-0008 [Accessed 8 Oct 2015].

50.   The effect of information overload on your consumers.. – Emarketingblog – blog on online marketing [online], 2015. Emarketingblog blog on online marketing. Available from:

http://emarketingblog.nl/2014/11/the-effect-of-information-overload-on-consumers/ [Accessed 8 Oct 2015].

51.   Why We Keep Playing the Lottery – Issue 17: Big Bangs – Nautilus [online], 2015. Nautilus. Available from:

http://nautil.us/issue/17/big-bangs/why-we-keep-playing-the-lottery-2 [Accessed 8 Oct 2015].

52.   How to Comprehend Incomprehensibly Large Numbers [online], 2015. io9. Available from:

http://io9.com/how-to-comprehend-incomprehensibly-large-numbers-1531604757 [Accessed 8 Oct 2015].

53.   WE Communications [online], 2015. WE Communications. Available from:

http://waggeneredstrom.com/what-we-do/social-innovation/report-digital-persuasion/ [Accessed 8 Oct 2015].

54.   To Increase Charitable Donations, Appeal to the Heart - Not the Head - Knowledge@Wharton [online], 2015. KnowledgeWharton To Increase Charitable Donations Appeal to the Heart Not the Head Comments. Available from:

http://knowledge.wharton.upenn.edu/article/to-increase-charitable-donations-appeal-to-the-heart-not-the-head/ [Accessed 21 Oct 2015].

55.   11 Obvious A/B Tests You Should Try [online], 2015. Quick Sprout. Available from:

   http://www.quicksprout.com/2013/01/14/11-obvious-ab-tests-you-should-try/ [Accessed 8 Oct 2015].

56.   Powell K.L., Roberts G. and Nettle D. (2012) Eye Images Increase Charitable Donations: Evidence From an Opportunistic Field Experiment in a Supermarket. Ethology, Vol 118 Issue 11. Available from:

   https://www.staff.ncl.ac.uk/daniel.nettle/PowellRobertsNettle.pdf

57.   Fathi M., Bateson M., and Nettle D. (2014). Effects of Watching Eyes and Norm Cues on Charitable Giving in a Surreptitious Behavioral Experiment. Evolutionary Psychology, 12 (5).

58.   Facebook Fundraising: Research You Can Use! – FrontStream [online], 2015. [online]. Facebook Fundraising: Research You Can Use! – FrontStream. Available from:

   http://info.frontstream.com/facebook-fundraising-whitepaper.html [Accessed 8 Oct 2015].

59.   2012: It Was a Very Good Year for Social Giving [Infographic] | Using Social Media for Charity | The Growing Trend in Social Giving | Crowdfunding Platforms [online], 2015. MDG Advertising. Available from:

   http://www.mdgadvertising.com/blog/2012-it-was-a-very-good-year-for-social-giving [Accessed 8 Oct 2015].

60.   Waggener Edstrom Worldwide Inc and Georgetown University (2012). Digital Persuasion:How social media motivates action and drives support. Available from:

   http://waggeneredstrom.com/downloads/DSCA-Summary.pdf. [Accessed 8 Oct 2015]

61.   The 2014 M R Benchmarks Study is Available for Download! [online], 2015.

[online]. M R 2014 Benchmarks. Available from:

http://mrbenchmarks.com/2014.html [Accessed 8 Oct 2015].

62.   The Surprising Secret to Higher Email Open Rates [online], 2014. The Daily Egg. Available from:

http://blog.crazyegg.com/2014/06/05/high-email-open-rates/ [Accessed 8 Oct 2015].

63.   Smith, S., Windmeijer, F. and Wright, E. (2015), Peer Effects in Charitable Giving: Evidence from the (Running) Field. The Economic Journal, 125: 1053–1071. doi: 10.1111/ecoj.12114. Available from:

http://onlinelibrary.wiley.com/doi/10.1111/ecoj.12114/full

64.   A world of good: JustGiving is transforming the charity sector through 'social giving' | Information Age [online], 2015. A world of good: JustGiving is transforming the charity sector through 'social giving' | Information Age. Available from:

http://www.information-age.com/industry/uk-industry/123459607/world-good-justgiving-transforming-charity-sector-through-social-giving [Accessed 8 Oct 2015].

65.   WE Communications [online], 2015. WE Communications. Available from:

http://waggeneredstrom.com/what-we-do/social-innovation/report-digital-persuasion/ [Accessed 8 Oct 2015].

66.   Optimization at the Obama campaign: a/b testing [online], 2015. Optimization at the Obama campaign: a/b testing. Available from:

http://kylerush.net/blog/optimization-at-the-obama-campaign-ab-testing/ [Accessed 8 Oct 2015].

67.   Matter of trust: what the public thinks of charities [online], 2015. New Philanthropy Capital (NPC). Available from:

http://www.thinknpc.org/publications/matter-of-trust/ [Accessed 8 Oct 2015].

68.   Jerwood, M. & Isaacs, K. (2014). 'The Psychology Of Online Giving'. Institute of Fundraising Technology Conference (Presentation).

69.   Optimising charity websites for donations [online], 2015. Optimising charity websites for donations. Available from:

https://www.eduserv.org.uk/insight/reports/optimising-charity-websites-for-donations [Accessed 8 Oct 2015].

70.   Jerwood, M. & Isaacs, K. (2014). 'The Psychology Of Online Giving'. Institute of Fundraising Technology Conference (Presentation).

71.   Latest news [online], 2015. Anthony Nolan. Available from:

http://www.anthonynolan.org/news/2015/08/04/twittercouple- astounded-followers-donate-over-£55000-week [Accessed 21 Oct 2015].

72.   NeverSeconds [online], 2015. NeverSeconds. Available from:

http://neverseconds.blogspot.co.uk/ [Accessed 8 Oct 2015].

73.   Quarter of charity funds now raised through online and mobile (Wired UK) [online], 2015. Wired UK. Available from:

http://www.wired.co.uk/news/archive/2013-11/27/charity-and-social-media [Accessed 21 Oct 2015].

74.   Ice Bucket Challenge to fund millions in research into motor neurone disease [online], 2015. [online]. MND Association. Available from:

http://www.mndassociation.org/news-and-events/latest-news/ice-bucket-announcement/ [Accessed 8 Oct 2015].

75.   Charity fundraising news - Over £11m raised for MND Association and Macmillan from ice bucket challenge [online], 2015. Civil Society. Available from:

http://www.civilsociety.co.uk/fundraising/news/content/18190/over_11m_raised_for_mnd_association_and_macmillan_from_ice_bucket_challenge [Accessed 8 Oct 2015]

76.   Record digital gifts to syria appeal [online], 2015. Civil Society. Available from:

http://www.civilsociety.co.uk/fundraising/news/content/18190/over_11m_raised_for_mnd_association_and_macmillan_from_ice_bucket_challenge [Accessed 8 Oct 2015]

About the Authors

Matt Haworth is one of the country's leading experts on doing good with digital. He's spent the last decade working with charities to help them raise funds and deliver more support online.

With Reason Digital, the digital innovation social enterprise he co-founded with Ed Cox in 2008, Matt has delivered digital fundraising projects and training for organisations including Age UK, Christian Aid, Alzheimer's Research UK, Save the Children, The Trussell Trust, the BBC, Virgin and many more. Matt, and the rest of the team at Reason Digital, regularly feature at conferences and in publications by the likes of The Guardian, The Media Trust, The Institute of Fundraising, CharityComms, Third Sector, Directory of Social Change, BBC, and others.

The team at Reason Digital includes co-authors Charlotte Taylor, Jordan Harling and Rebecca Rae; and researchers Ian Jukes and Paul Joyce. This book represents the best of their collective experience in making award winning digital fundraising campaigns, platforms and copy that delivers results for charities across a range of causes and organisations.

In 2015 Matt and Ed were jointly awarded the title of UK Digital Entrepreneur of the Year for their work with Reason Digital, recognising the increasingly vital role digital is playing in social good in the UK.

If you found this book helpful, have any suggestions, or just want to talk to the team at Reason Digital then we'd love to hear from you...

Get in touch

Web: www.reasondigital.com

Email: hello@reasondigital.com

Twitter: @ReasonDigital

Facebook: www.facebook.com/ReasonDigital

Tel: 0161 660 7949